Quality

KEYWORDS IN TEACHER EDUCATION

Series Editor: Viv Ellis

Taking cultural theorist Raymond Williams's concept as an organizing device, the **Keywords in Teacher Education** series offers short, accessibly written books on the most pressing and challenging ideas in the field.

Teacher education has a high profile in public policy and professional debates given the enduring associations between how teachers are prepared and how well their students do in school. At the same time, research perspectives on the important topics in the field are increasingly polarized with important consequences for the kind of teacher and the qualities of teaching that are most valued. Written by internationally recognized experts, these titles offer analyses both of the historical emergence and the consequences of the different positions in these debates.

Also Available in the Series:

Forthcoming in the series:

Quality

CLARE BROOKS

BLOOMSBURY ACADEMIC
LONDON · NEW YORK · OXFORD · NEW DELHI · SYDNEY

BLOOMSBURY ACADEMIC
Bloomsbury Publishing Plc
50 Bedford Square, London, WC1B 3DP, UK
1385 Broadway, New York, NY 10018, USA
29 Earlsfort Terrace, Dublin 2, Ireland

BLOOMSBURY, BLOOMSBURY ACADEMIC and the Diana logo are
trademarks of Bloomsbury Publishing Plc

First published in Great Britain 2023

Cover design by Charlotte James
Cover image © Zoonar GmbH / Alamy Stock Photo

A catalogue record for this book is available from the British Library.

A catalog record for this book is available from the Library of Congress.

ISBN: HB: 978-1-3502-8597-2
        PB: 978-1-3502-8596-5
        ePDF: 978-1-3502-8598-9
        eBook: 978-1-3502-8599-6

Series: Keywords in Teacher Education

Typeset by Integra Software Services Pvt. Ltd.
Printed and bound in Great Britain

To find out more about our authors and books visit www.bloomsbury.com
and sign up for our newsletters.

CONTENTS

FIGURES

TABLE

SERIES EDITOR'S FOREWORD

This series is organized by the concept of 'keywords', first elaborated by Welsh cultural theorist Raymond Williams (1976), and books in the series will seek to problematize and unsettle the ostensibly unproblematic and settled vocabulary of teacher education. From Williams's perspective, keywords are words and phrases that occur frequently in speech and writing, allowing conversation to ensue, but that nonetheless reveal profound differences in meaning within and across cultures, politics and histories. In teacher education, such keywords include practice, knowledge, quality and expertise. The analysis of such keywords allows us to trace the evolution of the emergent - and the maintenance of residual – meanings in teacher education discourses and practices. By analysing keywords, therefore, it is possible to elucidate the range of meanings of what Gallie (1955) referred to as 'essentially contested concepts' but in ways that promote a critical, historical understanding of changes in the fields in which they occur.

In the first edition of *Keywords*, Williams included entries on 108 units, ranging from 'Aesthetic' to 'Work'. A second edition followed in 1983 and other writers have subsequently used the concept to expand on Williams's original collection (e.g. Bennett et al., 2005; MacCabe and Yanacek, 2018) or to apply the concept to specific domains (e.g. A Community of Inquiry, 2018). This series applies it to teacher education. The purpose of the series mirrors that of Williams's original project: to trace ideological differences and social conflicts over time as they relate to the discourses and practices of a field (here, teacher education) by focusing on a selection of the field's high frequency words. So *Keywords in Teacher Education* is not a multi-volume dictionary.

The kind of analysis required by a focus on keywords goes beyond etymology or historical semantics. By selecting and analysing keywords, Williams argued:

> we find a history and complexity of meanings; conscious changes, or consciously different uses; innovation, obsolescence, specialization, extension, overlap, transfer; or changes which are masked by a nominal continuity so that words which seem to have been there for centuries, with continuous general meanings, have come in fact to express radically different or radically variable, yet sometimes hardly noticed, meanings and implications of meaning.
>
> (Williams, 1976, p. 17)

Given the increasingly strong attention paid to teacher education in education policy and in public debates about education more generally, focusing on keywords in this field is both timely and necessary. Uncovering and unsettling differences and conflicts in the vocabulary of preparing teachers renders the political and social bases underlying policy formation and public discourse more visible and therefore more capable of being acted upon.

Through this organizing device, the *Keywords in Teacher Education* series addresses the most important topics and questions in teacher education currently. It is a series of short books written in a direct and accessible style, each book taking one keyword as its point of departure and closely examining its cultural meanings historically whilst, crucially, identifying the social forces and material consequences of the differences and conflicts in meaning. Written by internationally recognized researchers, each peer-reviewed book offers cutting-edge analysis of the keyword underpinned by a deep knowledge of the available research within the field – and beyond it. One of the aims of the series is to broaden the gaze of teacher education research by engaging more systematically with the relevant humanities and social science literature – to acknowledge, as Williams did, that our understanding is deepened and potential for action strengthened by seeking to understand the social relations between words, texts and the multiple contexts in which their meanings are produced.

Who would not value 'quality'? Quality is not only a keyword (representing an essentially contested concept) but something of a cliché. It can trip off the tongue too easily, perhaps giving the speaker and writer a sense that they are on the right side of a 'debate' (as if anyone would advocate for 'sub-standard', for example). And it does trip off the tongue – the tongues of policy-makers and education reformers of all political colours and persuasions – applied to teachers as people (quality often simply meaning high-level prior academic qualifications) as well as their activities. Indeed, the slippage between 'quality' teachers and 'quality' teaching itself merits examination as it represents a crucially important distinction for what will always be a mass profession and one that distinguishes between measures of people (the 'right' sort of person allowed to become a teacher) and their work. 'Quality' as far as the teacher, is concerned, does not have an unblemished history with regards to equity and diversity. 'Quality' teaching is often defined in relation to ideological commitments just as it is to teachers' behaviours and their students' outcomes.

As Clare Brooks points out, in this excellent addition to the *Keywords in Teacher Education* series, the uses of 'quality' seem to have increased in frequency as policy-makers have become more influenced by economistic links between how school students perform in international assessments such as PISA and measures of economic productivity such as GDP. A belief has emerged that 'quality' in terms of teachers and teaching is something that policy-makers have control of and that make the biggest difference in terms of outcomes for students. And while it is generally accepted that the 'quality' of teaching is the most significant in-school factor affecting students' attainment and outcomes, the rhetorical intent of the 'quality' teachers and teaching discourse is to minimize the other social forces that make the biggest overall difference such as poverty. Brooks tackles the 'empty' and 'ill-defined' nature of the uses of 'quality' in the field of teacher education and shows how an expansive understanding of this important keyword can empower both teacher educators and their teacher students.

Viv Ellis
Melbourne, 2022

ACKNOWLEDGEMENTS

The research that underpins this book would not have been possible without the generosity and support of the many teacher educators who kindly agreed to take part in my research over the years, along with their colleagues, students and institutions who were generous in their access to their premises, students, partners and programmes. A special thanks goes to Elaine Sharpling for her insightful comments and support with the Welsh perspective.

CHAPTER ONE

Why Does Quality Teacher Education Matter So Much?

Why quality is a keyword for teacher education

In Raymond Williams's influential text on keywords, he identified a range of words in common usage that had specific complex meanings. Williams's text did much more than explore the etymology of these important words, but sought to cast light on their cultural meaning. In doing so, Williams sought to reveal the political struggles over the 'correct' meaning of a word, and how variations in interpretation can have far-reaching effects. 'Quality' is certainly such a word in teacher education where there is much discussion about its 'correct' meaning. How quality is defined in teacher education has significant scope to influence policy, practices and how teachers understand the expectations of them. Quality is in many respects a difficult concept to argue with (who wants poor-quality teacher education?). Approaches and initiatives are often prefixed with the word quality, used as an adjective, but without explanation of its precise meaning particularly in that context.

Everyone is united on the need for 'quality' teacher education, but there is little consensus as to what that might mean, what it looks like in practice, and who should contribute to that definition and debate. Indeed, one of the abiding issues in teacher education is that the universal focus for 'quality' appears to be driven by a range of international trends, national or regional policy initiatives, which are devolved away from the teacher educators who are responsible for it, and those in the school sector who have a vested interest in how new teachers are educated, trained and prepared. In other words, quality in teacher education can be seen as both a policy and a practice issue, which has a range of invested stakeholders and with little shared agreement as to what they understand quality to mean.

In this book, I unpack the different meanings and perspectives attributed to 'quality' in teacher education. I begin in this chapter with a focus on how quality has been interpreted differently over time and why quality has become such a dominant keyword in policy, practice and accountability related to teacher education. In Chapter 2, I outline research that has sought to define quality teacher education and review the pertinent messages and conundrums that emerge from that research. In Chapter 3, I explore different ways of judging quality through accountability measures, and the use of various measurements and metrics, and consider the impact and influence these can have on teacher education practices. Chapter 4 looks at two alternative approaches to quality teacher education: that of alternative provision and developing a research-orientation, and reviews the research that evaluates their success; and finally, Chapter 5 examines how teacher educators have adapted their practices in the light of various policy and accountability shifts in order to preserve, develop or maintain quality. Together the book explores the various different approaches and meanings attributed to quality teacher education and examines the implications of adopting these approaches.

At the outset, I want to be clear on what I am referring to when discussing quality related to teacher education.

Throughout this text, I focus on definitions, approaches and initiatives aimed at improving the quality of initial teacher education specifically. No doubt discussions around quality of teacher education are intimately related to debates around the quality of teaching and teacher quality. However, in the same way that it is often assumed that there is a relationship between quality teachers and quality teaching (or vice versa), it is important to be clear that it is an assumption that high-quality teacher education would result in the certification or qualification of high-quality teachers, or that graduates of such courses would teach well. However, high-quality teaching and high-quality teachers are not the focus of this particular text, although they will be referred to throughout. There are a number of factors that might influence their teaching once teachers graduate and become qualified, including factors pertinent to the teacher themselves, the school they work in and the context of that school, and especially the accountability measures that affects them. In other words, a teacher education programme alone will not determine whether someone is a good teacher or whether they are able to teach well. Other personal, school and community-related factors can affect individual teacher (or teaching) quality. This is not to say that the quality of a teacher education programme is irrelevant. Of course it is important, but there are significant other factors that may influence whether someone is seen to be a quality teacher or if they can teach well.

In this book, I also focus specifically on research focused on initial (or pre-service) teacher education. The examples and vignettes of practice are drawn from my own experience as a teacher educator, research collaborations with colleagues, and specifically draw upon research that I conducted between 2018 and 2020 on high-quality, large-scale teacher education programmes based in Arizona, United States; Auckland, New Zealand; Brisbane, Australia; London, England and Toronto, Canada (Brooks, 2021). I use these as examples of adaptive practices, but have also drawn upon the extensive literature in the field. Whilst I recognize that many, of the metrics, judgements and discourses around initial teacher education may apply to continuing professional development or in-service education, the emphasis is on the important aspects of quality that are significant at the start of a teacher's professional learning journey, recognizing that there may be some fundamentals pertinent to *initial* teacher education. Further professional development should be dependent on, and reflective of, the needs of the individual teacher and the school context and community they find themselves in. With that in mind, teacher education, unless otherwise stated, will refer to initial (or pre-service) teacher education.

Defining quality teacher education

In her discussion on teacher quality, Cochran-Smith (2021) notes two significant trends: firstly the link between teacher quality and economic performance that emerged from the McKinsey and Company report, where it was identified that teacher quality was the factor most open to policy influence (Barber & Mourshed, 2007). As Cochran-Smith notes, the impact of this logic: 'the quality of an education system cannot exceed the quality of its teachers' was extensive and influenced reports, speeches and policy documents around the globe. However, the mantra that 'teachers matter most' is based on a rather simplistic understanding of what teacher quality meant: largely taken from the economist's Hanushek's definition of teacher quality that good teachers are ones who get large gains in student achievement for their classes, and the logic that this should then be the focus of policy (Hanushek, 2002). Such simplistic perspectives can still be seen today. The *Next Steps: Report of the Quality of Initial Teacher Education Review* published in Australia (Paul, Louden, Elliott, & Scott, 2021) states that 'The aim of accredited ITE programs is to produce teachers who meet the Graduate level of the Teacher Standards and have the tools and knowledge to support students *in achieving a year's worth of academic growth in any given year'* (p. 37, my italics). In this way of defining quality, the purpose of teacher education, and indeed teaching is defined normatively, purely attributed to academic attainment.

When teacher quality is defined in this way, it negates the personal, social and cultural impact of education. Teacher quality is seen in narrow economic terms: in relation to the relationship between education and international competitiveness but also in relation to how that quality is judged: through a simplistic input-to-output logic. Such an empty approach to defining quality has been criticized in other aspects of education. For example, Tatto (2021) has criticized the dominance of econometric-based analysis in education policy making. Drawing upon the example of the United States, and specifically with reference to value-added methods (VAMs), she outlines how education policy agendas have become reliant on tools from econometric research, and are displacing educational research insights as the source of authoritative data to inform changes to both policy and practice. She also notes that educational research has not been able to respond to this shift. Econometric-based approaches conceptualize teaching in a way that belies the reality of the work that teachers do:

> A major concern is that these VAMs analysts are not immersed in the day-to-day task of teaching and learning or in preparing future teachers, and therefore lack the needed expertise and legitimacy to contribute in meaningful ways to the knowledge production that is needed to inform policy and practice by and for the teaching profession.
>
> (2021, p. 28)

Tatto's argument is that not only does this approach privilege research which is disconnected from practice, but that it is also constrained by a conception of education success solely orientated to achievement, a reliance on secondary data sets, and as such is severely limited. Whilst this not only has the impact of silencing the professional voices and expertise of the profession to determine its own knowledge base, it also runs the risk of defining quality in narrow terms, with a false veil of objectivity. Moreover, such research doesn't help to explain why some approaches to teacher education can be seen as 'quality' or better than others.

In order to understand quality teacher education, or to understand why some approaches are considered better quality than others (quality is often a comparative or relative judgement), it is important to consider how to think about quality in a way that is more aligned with education in the broader sense.

Quality within education

Lee Harvey's work in quality in the higher education sector (2007) distinguishes between quality and standards and argues that many definitions of quality are more aligned with quality assurance than an understanding of quality itself (see Table 1.1). He argues that quality and standards reference different aspects of education provision and are used for different purposes: quality assurance mechanisms do not (in themselves) enhance the provision of education, but are a process of governance, performing functions around accountability, control and compliance.

> Quality is to quality assurance what intelligence is to IQ tests. Quality, in higher education is, for example, about the nature of learning. Quality assurance is about convincing others about the adequacy of that processes of learning.
>
> (Harvey, 2007, p. 5)

Discussions on quality in education and teacher education tend to focus on the most appropriate metrics, and indicators which can be used to judge quality through outcomes, rather than to focus on learning itself (Bartell, Floden, & Richmond, 2018; Firestone & Donaldson, 2019; Gewirtz, Maguire, Neumann, & Towers, 2019; Skedsmo & Huber, 2019).

TABLE 1.1 Definitions of quality and standards (taken from Harvey, 2007).

Quality	Definition
Exceptional	A traditional concept linked to the idea of 'excellence', usually operationalized as exceptionally high standards of academic achievement. Quality is achieved if the standards are surpassed.
Perfection or consistency	Focuses on process and sets specifications that it aims to meet. Quality in this sense is summed up by the interrelated ideas of zero defects and getting things right the first time.
Fitness for purpose	Judges quality in terms of the extent to which a product or service meets its stated purpose. The purpose may be customer-defined to meet requirements or (in education) institution-defined to reflect institutional mission (or course objectives). *NB: There are some who suggest that 'fitness of purpose' is a definition of quality but it is a specification of parameters of fitness and not itself a definition of the quality concept.*
Value for money	Assesses quality in terms of return on investment or expenditure. At the heart of the value-for-money approach in education is the notion of accountability. Public services, including education, are expected to be accountable to the funders. Increasingly, students are also considering their own investment in higher education in value-for-money terms.
Transformation	Sees quality as a process of change, which in higher education adds value to students through their learning experience. Education is not a service for a customer but an ongoing process of transformation of the participant. This leads to two notions of transformative quality in education: enhancing the consumer and empowering the consumer.

Quality	Definition
Standards	
Academic standards	The demonstrated ability to meet specified level of academic attainment. For pedagogy, the ability of students to be able to do those things designated as appropriate at a given level of education. Usually, the measured competence of an individual in attaining specified (or implied) course aims and objectives, operationalized via performance on assessed pieces of work. For research, the ability to undertake effective scholarship or produce new knowledge, which is assessed via peer recognition.
Standards of competence	Demonstration that a specified level of ability on a range of competencies has been achieved. Competencies may include general transferable skills required by employers; academic ('higher level') skills implicit or explicit in the attainment of degree status or in a post-graduation academic apprenticeship; particular abilities congruent with induction into a profession.
Service standards	Are measures devised to assess identified elements of the service provided against specified benchmarks? Elements assessed include activities of service providers and facilities within which the service takes place. Benchmarks specified in 'contracts' such as student charters tend to be quantified and restricted to measurable items. *Post hoc* measurement of customer opinions (satisfaction) is used as indicators of service provision. Thus, service standards in higher education parallel consumer standards.
Organizational standards	Attainment of formal recognition of systems to ensure effective management of organizational processes and clear dissemination of organizational practices.

With high levels of governance and oversight, teacher education is prone to certain definitions of quality which are easier to define in terms of quality assurance (or standards), as they lead to metrics, measures and indicators more readily (these are discussed in more detail in Chapter 3). Other dimensions of quality, such as transformation, are more difficult to quantify as they are less observable, less immediate in terms of impact and more personal to the individual (Evans, 2011; Halász & Looney, 2019). Harvey argues that this difficulty in measurement should not mean that they get forgotten (approaches which seek to take a different view on quality are outlined in Chapters 4 and 5).

However, discussions about quality in teacher education are not always clear on how quality is being defined: it is often left as an empty concept. The simple conception that quality is somehow measurable and observable, through the results of outcomes of teaching (or for teacher education: the outcomes for the students as a result of the teachers) has been widely critiqued. As Biesta and colleagues have argued (2021), the logical of the market is not the logic of education, and the consequences of using a market rationale and focusing on indicators and metrics to show added value are in effect 'anti-educational' (because they divert attention towards that which is being measured). This is also reflected in the experience of new teachers who can experience tension between the official definitions of quality and what they realize is important for their development (Sullivan, 2020).

The ubiquitous use of the word 'quality' is such that it has become an ill-defined adjective (Alexander, 2015), tagged onto an activity (quality teaching, quality learning) without a clear sense of what it is that warrants its use. In some cases, quality is used as a slogan to show that something is somehow 'better' although in what ways better is being conceived is absent or poorly defined (Biesta et al., 2021).

Harvey's categorization breaks down different ways in which the word can be used and what that might refer to. For example, achievement against a set of Teacher Standards (standards of competency), or high scores in student satisfaction surveys (service standards) can both be used as monikers of 'quality' but reflect different perspectives of what is valued or what is considered important: a course that rates highly on service standards might have satisfied students but this does not mean that they can teach well (although it is likely that if they can't teach well, they may not be so satisfied!). In other words, focusing on some standards more than others reflects what is being valued rather than a clear indication that some standards are inherently 'better' than others or that they are more illuminative of quality teacher education. Quality is often used in such relative terms highlighting that some approaches may lead to higher performance in certain metrics. However, it would be misleading to suggest that there is a magic formula or definition of quality teacher education that applies in all contexts and to all circumstances. Quality is used variously, belying different conceptions, interpretations and meanings.

Some courses or programmes that are considered to be high quality rely on notions of exceptionality or excellence: such as through having high entry requirements or rigorous entry assessments. Harvey notes that quality may be interpreted as exclusivity or exceptionality, and this may be due to being associated with a prestigious institution. In which case, quality here may be more related to perceptions and access to social networks rather than the transformational nature of the learning experience on offer.

In other words, when we discuss quality in teacher education, it is important to explore the underpinning assumptions about why something is being privileged as 'quality'. To suggest that quality can be determined by achieving a range of (professional) Standards suggests a linear relationship: that those Standards are in themselves an authoritative account of better quality, which reveals:

> an explicit view that complying with requirements will result in competent graduates, a process that can be checked through measurable, observable variables.
>
> (Harvey, 2007, p. 13)

This claim can, of course, be challenged. Sleeter (2019) notes how definitions of quality are likely to be defined by those that have power. Others have argued that teacher educators should 'reclaim accountability' and foreground alternative values such as democracy and social justice (Cochran-Smith et al., 2018), or to focus on the 'core practices' or classroom behaviours that teachers need (Grossman, 2018; Grossman, Kavanagh, & Dean, 2018; Grossman & Pupik Dean, 2019). These arguments whilst avoiding the limiting conception of standards are still unable to fully describe what it is about a high-quality teacher education programme or course that has the potential to transform someone into a teacher.

Quality teacher education as transformation

Biesta (2012) argues that in order to understand quality, it is necessary to have a conception of education. If education is conceived in narrow attainment terms (the passing of exams for example), then quality will be judged in relation to whether the attainment goals have been reached. A broader conception of education where it is seen as opening up, rather than closing down, is more aligned with Biesta's term of transcendence, and this requires a very different conception of quality such as that which Harvey describes as transformation.

Transformation has often been used in relation to learning, particularly adult learning in higher education, see for example, Mezirow's ideas of transformational learning (2000) and Netolicky's (2019) conception of transformational professional learning. Transformation within education implies change in the person who is being educated: a change that is so significant that it results in that person's emancipation and empowerment. Such a change requires an assessment and re-evaluation of currently held beliefs and actions. It is through an educative process that those beliefs and actions undertake a change in form. The process of education does not necessarily prescribe what this change of form may be, but it is necessary for it to occur for the process to be considered *educational* (Harvey & Knight, 1996).

The idea of transformation has been widely taken up in some part of the higher education community, and has been used in teacher education as a way of supporting an activist orientation. For example, Kennedy (2018) describes a teacher education programme orientated around the idea of transformation, drawing on Sach's (2003) idea of the activist professional. Kennedy highlights that this approach enables new teachers to engage in a professionally authentic experience where they are supported in taking responsibility for their own learning, working as part of both university and school communities throughout their programme, enabling genuine integration of theory and practice (more on this in Chapter 5). This reflects Harvey's idea of transformation as a definition of quality: changing the form of someone who is not a teacher, into that of being a teacher. Quality teacher education seen as transformation goes beyond proxy measures such as completion and employment rates but embraces a broader educational perspective related to the professional expectations of teachers.

Adopting transformation as a marker for quality in initial teacher education is not without its challenges. Whilst in many places the process of qualifying to become a teacher means meeting certain prescribed competence criteria or professional standards, this may not align with the less-prescriptive goal of transformation. Also, because transformation is an internal process that involves change, it is difficult to observe, account for or to measure. The process or outcomes of transformation may not be visible:

> [B]ecause there are no simple indicators, no self-evident or taken-for-granted and easily assimilated criteria for judging how students are empowered as critical reflective learners.
> (Harvey, 2007, p. 10)

However, without transformation, a programme merely teaches *about* teaching, rather than supporting individuals to *become* teachers.

A key theme throughout this book is that when quality is confused with accountability, and when teacher educators are compelled to comply with accountability measures, then it becomes difficult to plan for transformation: it is, in effect, anti-educational. Teacher educators often find they have to work around or subvert accountability measures which get in the way of transformative practices (as outlined in Chapter 5). These teacher educators understand that transformation requires a qualitative change in form, and as Harvey and Knight (1996) argue, this requires enhancing and empowering the participant. An overly prescriptive legislative and regulatory structure can prevent teacher education programmes and teacher educators from exercising such autonomy.

Why is quality teacher education an issue?

Having established that there are different ways of thinking about quality, it is important to consider why quality has become such a dominant discussion topic in and around teacher education. On one hand, this can be seen as a common-sense issue: who would argue for bad quality teacher education? The drive for policies that promote quality teacher education is also not new: in England, quality have featured in the title of policy White papers as far back as 1983 and 1987. But more recently, there has been a widespread growth in concern about quality in relation to teacher education, teachers and teaching, which Cochran-Smith (2021) notes became 'common parlance in the international discourse of education policy generally, and in particular, in discussions related to teaching standards, teacher evaluation policy and practice, teacher preparation practice and policy, and comparisons of education systems' (p. 416).

As already noted there are two drivers that are often cited when making the case for improvements in or further consideration of quality:

- Quality education is important for economic growth, and international competitiveness in this area, influenced by the rise of international league tables such as PISA and TIMSS, has resulted in concerns about countries being 'left behind' in those international league tables. Ball (2003) notes how this is often achieved through a narrative of crisis, which is used to justify the need for urgent action: a factor that Barnes (2021) illustrates is rife particularly in the Australian media.

- Quality teachers are the one area that can be influenced by policy, as suggested in the McKinsey and Company report.

In both of these arguments there is a simplistic logic that quality teachers are important for a quality education (which in turn will promote economic competitiveness), and that the key to having quality teachers is to ensure they are developed through a quality teacher education (note, here the emphasis on quality teachers rather than quality teaching). Not only has the evidence and the data which underpins this argument been questioned (see Pachler, 2013 and Jerrim, 2011), but also the McKinsey and Company report (Barber & Mourshed, 2007) on which this argument is often based, actually states that the largest variation in outcomes is attributable to social background and the students themselves, but the most important influence 'potentially open to policy influence' is teaching, and especially 'teacher quality' (OECD, 2005, p. 26).

There are two aspects of this statement that are particularly noteworthy. The first one, highlighted by Connell (2009), is that the statement suggests that the OECD do not consider social factors to be within policy influence, and place the policy initiative on teachers rather than on other societal factors. The second is that by focusing on teachers, the statement directs attention away from other important parts of the education system. Teachers are not alone in deciding how they undertake their work. Teaching is subject to a range of influences and controls: inspection regimes, testing, reward structures, managerial interventions. Intentionally or not, these affect teachers' work. Saying that teachers are the most influential factor focuses the attention on discussions about improving education, and educational disadvantage firmly onto teachers, making them the 'subject of reform' (Ball, 2008). To focus the attention onto teachers, and the quality of teachers onto teacher educators, has the effect of ignoring or downplaying the role that the infrastructure, policy effects, society and wider influences around teachers and schools can play in creating the conditions in which they undertake their work.

However, it is also the case that there are a number of concerns raised by both current and practising teachers and schools that teacher education needs to be improved because newly qualified teachers are underprepared to undertake the work expected of them. This may be attributed to the approaches or theories which underpin current teacher education practices, but is often also combined with an argument that teacher education would be better if it was removed from universities into more practice-based settings (more on this in Chapter 4). Underpinning this argument is a concern that teacher education (particularly when university based) is too widely removed from teaching.

Cochran-Smith and colleagues (2020) show that when this argument is made it presents teacher education as a problem. This problem may be attributed to deficiencies in regulation, or in accountability (both of which are then solved through the introduction of more accountability measures); or it is attributed to the configuration of a programme and how it links theory to practice. Not only are these arguments highly contested, but they are based on different notions of effectiveness, different ideas of schooling and different reasoning in logic. However, concerns about the relationship between theory and practice within teacher education have a long genealogy (Richert, 1997), and appear to be a perennial concern.

There have been concerns expressed about preparing teachers in universities, sites distant from the practice of classrooms. In most systems, teacher education has been a fairly recent introduction to the university system (Moon, 2016), and as Labaree (2006) notes, it has never really sat comfortably within the academy. Internationally, moving teacher education into universities from Teachers Colleges and Normal Schools was intended to professionalize teaching and raise its status. The promise of close proximity with educational research was hoped to professionalize teaching and to raise its status, thereby attracting higher qualified entrants. However, moving teacher education into universities has not always yielded the promised results, and where entry levels have increased, attempts to raise the status of teachers have been come into conflict with the need to use non-qualified or emergency-certified teachers in order to the meet demand for new teachers. Teaching is still seen as a profession of low status, if indeed it is considered a profession at all.

The concern about university-based teacher education is that it produces inadequate teachers because it is disconnected from practice, and is overly theoretical (as in the argument outlined in the Holmes Group report, 1986). This became a high-profile debate as key figures joined in the discussion such as Arthur Levine (from Teachers College) and Arne Duncan (education advisor to President Obama). At that time, and even today, newly qualified teachers can be critical of their teacher education, as they feel ill-prepared when they start their careers. However, the public debate on the quality of university-based teacher education has been staunchly defended by Zeichner (2017) as being politically motivated and subject to what he has described as the misquoting of evidence, echo chambers and knowledge ventriloquism.

However, even if such concerns are politically motivated, the issues they raise warrant further attention. Zeichner (2017) acknowledges that there are wide variations in the quality of teacher education provision across universities, and Goldhaber (2018) acknowledges that there may be some empirical evidence to the criticisms raised. Across the university sector there is a recognition that teacher education is not always as good as we would like it to be (Teacher Education Exchange, 2017), and that there is room for improvement. But there is a relationship between the regulations and accountability measures which can limit or confine what is possible within teacher education programmes, which are often attributed to factors outside of university provider's control such as the limited period of time allowed to become a teacher, or the assessment mechanisms that are prescribed for use. Also, as Zeichner highlights, this is not an even playing field: non-university-based providers can access private and public monies, such as those raised from venture philanthropy, which are not matched by public funding and which are not available to universities. Therefore, opportunities for innovation, development, alternative forms of school partnerships are not always possible. Zeichner, in relation to the United States, argues that the focus of the criticisms, and the hostile funding environment privileges alternative providers.

Although the situation is more advanced in the United States, similar trends can be seen elsewhere. The 1998 Hillage Report (Hillage, Pearson, Anderson, & Tamkin, 1998) noted similar concerns with university-based teacher education in England, which was also seen as being over-theorized, fragmented and unhelpful for teacher's professional practice. Traditionally, in England, the defence of university-based teacher education has been formulated around its proximity to research. However, the Carter Review in 2015 highlighted that even in research-intensive universities, researchers were not fully engaged in teacher education programmes. It is also true to note, as Pring (2017) does, that the research that has had substantial impact on teaching (he uses the examples of the impact of social disadvantage, quantitative analysis and the uses of IQ tests) has often come from other faculties outside (teacher) education.

In England, hostility towards university-based teacher education has taken a particular shape and form as the former Secretary of State for Education, Michael Gove described such teacher educators as 'the Blob' and the 'enemies of promise', contributing to what Furlong refers to (using a phrase from Ball, 1990) as the 'discourse of derision' (Furlong, 2019). Successive education policies have deliberately sought to foreground school-led teacher education designed to destabilize and decentre universities from teacher education (Department for Education, 2010), and these have been confounded recently by a wholescale review of what the Department for Education has called an ITT (Initial Teacher Training) Market Review (Department for Education, 2021). Interestingly, in response to this review there was sector-wide condemnation of both the review and the need for all providers to seek re-accreditation to be teacher education providers, but until this point, universities have been somewhat passive in their response to criticisms and policy shifts, leaving some to call for a re-invigorated approach to teacher education (Ellis, Souto-Manning, & Turvey, 2018; Teacher Education Exchange, 2017).

Similar trends can be seen in Australia and elsewhere. Connell (2009), Ling (2017) and Sachs (2015) have highlighted the same trends across Australia, and policy papers make reference to similar concerns in New Zealand (2017). Back in 2008, Grossman warned that if teacher educators failed to take these criticisms seriously, other organizations would seek to replace the universities' monopoly on the preparation of teachers. Such trends are symptomatic with marketization and centralization of control which Mayer has described as neoliberal education policies (2017). The language of neoliberalism ties up such approaches by using seemingly benign terms: marketization, choice, deregulation and accountability. But these policies are not benign: they contribute to an increasingly hostile climate for universities involved in teacher education, who are often ill-prepared to respond. Perhaps more worryingly, they take the debate about quality teacher education outside of those that are responsible for it (universities and schools), and place it in the hands of policy makers and policy influencers.

In other parts of the world, the challenges of teacher education are all too familiar: concerns about teacher quality, problems with teacher recruitment and the supply of quality teachers particularly to rural or remote communities is widespread across a whole range of countries in the Global South. Tao (2016) argues that teachers in the Global South are often portrayed as deficient, unreliable and unprofessional, but that such accounts do not consider the ways in which teachers' behaviours and capabilities are constrained, and how this is often linked to wider issues, such as gender inequality, rural education needs, poverty and adequate infrastructure. Global organizations like UNESCO have a number of initiatives around teacher status, that involve the use of normative instruments, and teacher policies and strategies which are designed to support teacher education and the quality of teaching.

However, these trends and approaches can be seen as part of what Sahlberg referred to as the Global Education Reform Movement (GERM) (Sahlberg, 2010). As Mayer (2017) notes, this has resulted in a commonality in education policy based on a limited repertoire of policy interventions which have been widely adopted internationally. Interventions aimed at addressing teacher quality include the introduction and dominance of Teacher Standards, accreditation procedures for teacher education providers and the provision of inspection regimes. These make up what Ball (2008) describes as technologies of performativity that lead to patterns of governance rather than government. In other words, rather than being strategies that improve the quality of teacher education, they become ways of governing teacher education and narrowing how it is discussed. When benchmarks are used to judge teacher education, the impact can be to lower the expectations for programmes that go beyond this benchmark, or to prevent the development of innovative approaches to teacher education which do not conform to a narrow and prescriptive norm. Whilst the deregulation of teacher education combined with a centralization of accreditation potentially opens up teacher education to new and alternative approaches (as seen in several international contexts), the consequence is the growth of global movements such as those aligned with the Teach for All network which, despite having some positives, also have dubious records of success and poor records of retention (Ellis et al., 2015; Thomas, Rauschenberger, & Crawford-Garrett, 2020).

At the same time, the influence and number of stakeholders who now have a vested interest in teacher education provision has increased, a situation that Ling, in relation to Australia has described as one of supercomplexity (2017). Schools have been long-standing partners with universities in teacher education. Teacher education is now often overseen by various regulatory bodies: sometimes government departments for education at a state or national level. Teacher standards and accreditation processes may be 'owned' by these bodies or certification councils, bodies or professional associations. These organizations have wide-ranging powers influencing the content, approach, assessment and formation of a teacher education programme. In addition, there is increasing complexity in accrediting who becomes a provider of teacher education, who condones and awards the qualification for individual teacher candidates, and who inspects and regulates the provision. And there is little evidence that this complexity has led to substantial increases in quality.

These complex webs of stakeholders and the wide use of accountability measures have focused on teachers and teacher education, to use Ball's term, as the 'subject for reform'. All of these infrastructural and governance concerns are tied up with ideological and political pressures which promote particular views of teacher education, and which permeate not just the public discourse about teacher education, but also the ways in which teacher education has been subjected to policies of reform. Accountability regimes that have now become a ubiquitous part of the teacher education landscape which underplay important values around democracy, equity and social justice, and focus on narrow outcomes measures described as 'attainment'. They dominate discussions about quality and how it is defined,

In the light of these reforms, how we understand quality in teacher education has also changed as it varies in how it is described, judged, evaluated and reassessed. As the chapters in this book will go on to explore, our understanding of teacher education has changed as discourses around quality have focused attention on a few narrow elements, responding in a limited way to the criticisms held against it. In this sense, I have described quality in teacher education as a conundrum (Brooks, 2021), or a tricky problem that can skew or influence practices with the intention of improving practice, but that can have perverse effects. This is the case of approaches which are too narrowly focused on problems of teacher supply, or that focus on measuring quality, which can divert practices away from transformation. Therefore, this book focuses on key questions around quality, but in doing so it acknowledges that the answers to those questions are probably different depending on the viewpoint of different stakeholders and what they value.

A central message throughout this book then is how teacher educators can be empowered, so that their adaptivity is recognized as being key to influence quality and is also limited by what is beyond their control. This is not to ignore the systemic influences that can influence an important practice like teacher education but to highlight the agency that teacher educators have and can use in the light of the various influences and initiatives that are designed to influence their work.

CHAPTER TWO

What Makes for Quality Teacher Education?

Chapter 1 highlighted that quality in teacher education was often poorly defined, highly contextual, and used relatively with a variety of different meanings. There have been a number of reviews that have sought to categorize and synthesize the distinctive features that will determine quality teacher education, although these are often commissioned by, or related to, policy reforms and reviews (Hulme, Rauschenberger, & Meanwell, 2018). The quality of such reviews themselves is often questioned as reflected in Louden's article title: *101 damnations: the persistence of criticism and the absence of evidence about teacher education in Australia* (2008).

Many of these reviews and summaries note that it is difficult to draw conclusions about effective teacher education programmes due to the number of variables related to it (not least the previous educational background and experience of teacher education candidates, and the partnership arrangements with placements schools). In fact, as Menter et al. (2010) note, the research basis for these reviews is often 'fragmented and non-cumulative, with a high volume of "one off" single cohort studies'. Consequently, they go on to argue that there is little evaluative research in teacher education, and quote Kirby and colleagues who says that 'While rife with rhetoric and innovative ideas, teacher education reform is sadly short on objective evaluations' (Kirby, McCombs, Barney, & Naftel, 2006, p. 25).

However, Darling-Hammond and her colleagues (Darling-Hammond, 2006, 2017, 2021; Darling-Hammond et al., 2000) have conducted various reviews into teacher education programmes which were chosen following an extensive collection of evidence of their high quality from practitioners, scholars, employers and graduates, the findings of which have gained wide traction. Their study of well-reputed US-based programmes determined a range of common features, which were further expanded by their later international study which identified the following characteristics:

- Coherence, based on a common vision of good teaching grounded in an understanding of learning and permeating all coursework and clinical experiences.

- A strong core curriculum, taught in the context of practice and grounded in knowledge of child and adolescent development, learning in social and cultural contexts, curriculum, assessment and subject-matter pedagogy.

- Extensive, connected clinical experiences, carefully developed to support the ideas and practices presented in simultaneous, closely interwoven coursework.

- Well-defined standards of professional knowledge and practice, used to guide and evaluate coursework and clinical work.

- Explicit strategies, to help students confront their own deep-seated beliefs and assumptions about learning, and learn about the experiences of other people.

- An inquiry approach that connects theory and practice – e.g. 'action research' and related approaches (which engages teachers in research and analysis of their own practice and includes cycles of reflection and improvement).

- Strong school–university partnerships, to develop common knowledge and shared beliefs among school-based and university-based faculty, allowing candidates to learn to teach in professional communities that model state-of-the-art practice for diverse learners and collegial learning for adults.

- Assessment based on professional standards, to evaluate teaching through demonstration of critical skills and abilities using performance assessments and portfolios supporting the development of 'adaptive expertise' (Darling-Hammond, 2006, p. 276).

These factors were summarized by Hammerness and Klette (2015) into three categories, and through an exploration of the range of international empirical evidence on quality indicators, they established a list of indicators that related to Vision, Coherence and Opportunities to enact practice as summarized below. Indicators of vision referred to:

- An explicit vision of good teaching

- Which is elaborated and specific

- Known and understood by faculty and students

- Relates to specific strategies or teaching approaches

Coherence refers to that which links theory and practices and is indicated by:

- How the vision informs the opportunities to learn in the program

- Awareness and understanding by both faculty and students, who also agree to and value the vision

- Course content communicates similar ideas about teaching and learning and require students to link theory and practice

- Practicum where the student teacher draws upon the
  university programme and the university programme
  draws upon the practical experiences from schools.

Opportunities to enact practice are indicated through:

- Planning for and enactment of teaching and the role of
  being a teacher
- Analysis of pupil learning, and awareness of their
  perspectives
- Consideration of teaching materials and resources
- Conversations about the school placement experiences
  and student teaching
- Visible connections with models of teaching and
  national and local curriculums and contexts.

Hammerness and Klette were able to use these key indicators
to analyse how different teacher education programmes sought
to connect theory and practice: listing a range of practices they
included. However, Hammerness and Klette point out that these
are only elements of what has been included in a programme,
and as indicators they do not offer a conceptualization of
quality. In other words, they argue that their data did not
reveal the quality of the opportunity, but the likelihood that
it exists. This is a key finding for any synthesis of research
into quality practices, as just because opportunities to learn are
present does not mean that they have the anticipated impact
on the learners, or that they are indicative of high-quality (or
transformative) educative practices.

This finding is corroborated by other research that has
sought to compare different approaches to teacher education.
For example, in their review of the quality and effectiveness
of programmes considered to be alternative provision, Ing
and Loeb (2008) note that attributing quality to individual
measures or programme elements (such as programme design,

partnership placement or the characteristics of the teacher candidates) is not possible, as each indicator can outweigh the impact of the others. For them the success of a programme relates to the ways in which individual experiences are supported and offset: so adjustments can be made for the individual candidate, the programme curriculum, or the placement school setting. In other words, they suggest that quality or effectiveness is when programmes are responsive to the needs, progress and attainment of the individual.

Most teacher education programmes consist of a similar array of activities or learning opportunities, including to a greater or lesser extent the following activities:

- Taught sessions/workshops

- Classroom experience

- Activities that reflect approximations of practice (see Grossman, 2018)

- Teaching practice

- Mentoring

- Formative feedback

- Summative feedback

- Lesson observations

- Assignments/assessment

- Portfolios

- Reflective activities

The quality of a programme will depend on how these elements interact with each other which in turn will be underpinned by the coherence of the vision of education. It will also depend on the quality of the experiences themselves and the support offered to individuals to help them to make sense of them. In other words, whilst they present opportunities to learn, their presence does not in itself equate to quality teacher education, or a transformative experience. The factors of vision and coherence will attest to how well these elements combine within a programme, but the quality of that programme will also relate to the extent to which the learning experiences align with the particular needs of the individual and the context they find themselves in.

Identifying teacher education practices as 'core'

Chapter 1 made reference to the argument that teacher education needed to improve because new teachers felt inadequately prepared for the classroom. Therefore, one way of viewing the particular elements of a teacher education programme is through this lens: how does it prepare new teachers for the classroom, and what is the evidence that some approaches do this better than others?

In England, in response to the English government's publication of an series of recommendations from their own Expert Group on the Market Review of initial teacher training, and the responding criticism of the lack of evidence underpinning this report, Sam Sims, an economist published an essay (2021) where he argued that research orientated around practice-based teacher education has been the best evidence of a quality approach to teacher education, which he argues has shown 'how it is possible to integrate theory and practice in a way that respects the situated and sophisticated nature of teachers' work' (p. 29). In a follow-up conversation with Sims, he noted that this was based on his reading of the research, as he did not have any first-hand experience of teaching or teacher education, nor had he worked with teacher educators in his own institution in forming this view. The body of evidence that he refers to is drawn almost exclusively from the work of Grossman and her colleagues on core practices

(Grossman, 2018), and reflects the body of work undertaken under the banner of the core practices.

The need for a consensus about the form and process of teacher education has been made for some time (Cochran-Smith, 2004, 2005; Cochran-Smith & Zeichner, 2005; Hiebert, Gallimore, & Stigler, 2002). Grossman, Hammerness and McDonald (2009) argued that teacher education needed a common language around core practices that would help to address common issues such as the separation of methods and foundations courses (or theory and practice courses) which can lead to a disconnect between work undertaken on the programme with that in the practical school experience. They also argued it would address the need to integrate practices throughout teacher education programmes; and the need to resituate practice to be at the core of the teacher education curriculum. Their research builds on the scholarship developed from subject-based investigations into pedagogical content knowledge, collated from TeachingWorks' and other frameworks from University of Michigan, Core Practice Consortium, CSET at Stanford, and University of Washington's Ambitious Science Teaching Project.

They describe the findings of this work as comprising high-leverage practices: research-based, and effective practices that could be used frequently and widely to support novices' understanding and progress. This body of work has been developed into a series of approaches for teacher education which they argue could be used to support the development of core practices: through representations and approximations of practice, achieved through strategies such as modelling and rehearsal (Grossman, 2018), and supported by a range of research into the practices into how those core practices can be adopted and used (Anderson & Herr, 2011; Grossman, Kazemi, Kavanagh, Franke, & Dutro, 2019; Grossman & Pupik Dean, 2019; O'Flaherty & Beal, 2018; Van Der Schaaf, Slof, Boven, & De Jong, 2019).

The aim of this work is commendable as it seeks to go to the heart of the theory-practice division so often the critique of teacher education programmes, and to focus on the classroom practice and behaviours of new teachers. However, it is important to recognize what this approach can contribute to quality teacher education experiences and what it omits. The teaching strategies it promotes include representations and approximations of practice, to which new teachers are encouraged to learn through strategies such as modelling and rehearsal. Necessarily then, this focuses on particular classroom behaviours that teachers can rehearse, try out, amend and adopt. But an over-emphasis on teacher behaviours can represent a narrow and technical view of teaching, that focuses on what the teacher does in the classroom, rather than the relationships and interactions they need to build with students.

Whilst it was not the intention of the core practice movement that this should be the sole focus of teacher education programmes, there is a danger that conducting teacher education only in this way represents a simplistic understanding of what constitutes teaching (Jones & Ellis, 2019). As an illustrative example, the 'teacher moves' developed by Lemov (2010) are based on his experience and observations of 'effective' teacher behaviours. New teachers often ask for more practical tips about teaching and books such as Lemov's *Teach like a Champion* which focus exclusively on teachers' behaviour are incredibly popular. However, the thinking, understanding, concepts and ideas that underpin these behaviours are largely invisible, as they focus explicitly on the visible part of teaching: what teachers do in the classroom: techniques, routines and behaviours. Developing a set of techniques and routines is important for any teacher: but an exclusive focus on them as part of a teacher education programme erroneously suggests that teaching is predominantly a set of skills, and that teacher education should focus on the rehearsal and adoption of these skills. Philip et al. (2018) have been particularly critical of this approach, describing it as focusing on prescriptive practices, focusing on behaviours and not on issues of justice and equity. Similarly, Barnes, Quiñones and Berger (2021) have noted that there is a paucity of evidence around the efficacy of high-leverage practices, particularly for early years education.

The idea that teacher development should be based on this 'simple' view is symptomatic of the view which Labaree summarized as: 'teaching is a complex job that looks deceptively simple' (2006). Most adults have gone through some form of formal education, and have an image of what teaching looks like, enshrined in images and metaphors from our own 'apprenticeship of observation' (Lortie, 1975) as a pupil. These images are reinforced through media representations of teaching (Henry, 2020; Moore, 2004), which new teachers may seek to replicate. There is a misconception that all teaching requires is the development of these familiar behaviours by someone with adequate (subject) knowledge, and that teacher education should consist merely of the development of this 'craft' knowledge of behaviours. Tatto, Richmond and Carter Andrews (2016) suggest that the discourse around minimalist teacher education is based on the idea that as long as teachers are prepared in their subjects, learning to teach only requires a short period of induction. Whilst they argue that this runs counter to the research evidence, they argue that this places an over-emphasis on technical practice which is reductionist and does not prepare teachers well to practice the moral-ethical judgements, and creative problem solving they need. An over-reliance on prescribed procedures and rule-following can lead to inappropriate action, or teaching that is performative and managerialist (Edwards-Groves & Grootenboer, 2015).

This argument aligns with the distinction that Orchard and Winch (2015) make in their philosophical account of different approaches to the education of teachers. Orchard and Winch distinguish between seeing teachers as executive technicians ('told prescriptively by others what to do, without needing to understand why they are being told to do it'), craft workers or professionals:

> The teacher who is able to engage with theory and the findings of educational research shares with the craft worker teacher a capacity for self-direction. By contrast, though, the professional teacher is able to judge right action in various school and classroom contexts from a more reliable basis

for judgment than intuition or common sense. A teacher who is able to make good situational judgments does not rely on hearsay or unreflective prejudice. She draws on a well-thought-through and coherent conceptual framework, on knowledge of well-substantiated empirical research, and on considered ethical principles, to arrive at decisions in the classroom context.

(Orchârd & Winch, 2015, p. 14)

This idea of having the knowledge in order to make good and ethical situational judgements necessitates a teacher education which is more expansive than one which focuses solely on practice or behaviours. This is not to say, of course, that a focus on what teachers do in the classroom, and being able to teach effectively should not be part of a quality teacher education experience.

Approaches reflecting clinical practice

Whilst the techniques outlined in the core practice movement can help with connecting theory and practice in classroom behaviours, quality teacher education needs to go further and to develop the knowledge and understanding needed for situational judgement. One approach that seeks to achieve this, and has received widespread support is that of clinical practice. In the BERA/RSA *Review of 'Research-informed clinical practice' in initial teacher education* Burn and Mutton (2013) review models of clinical practice in teacher education including the Teachers for a New Era programme, the Melbourne Master of Teaching and Realistic or 'realistic' or 'authentic' teacher education in the Netherlands, and the Finnish model that integrates research. In their review they recognize that teacher education must move beyond decontextualized research-based understandings of practice, or a limited range of classroom experience, to an approach that recognizes the complexity and context-specific nature of experienced teachers' knowledge and experience, and builds upon that experience alongside, and with the support of, those experienced teachers and communities of practice. Whilst they recognize that direct correlations between this approach and the success of education systems such as that experienced in Finland can only be inferred, they do argue that the research orientation required of all qualified teachers equips them to continue developing their practice in response to new challenges. Being able to evaluate the findings of wider academic research can have a positive impact on their practice, which in turn can be analysed in terms of the student experience and outcomes. In the Netherlands they argue that analysis has shown a positive relationship between features of the programme – such as the tight integration and careful graduation of tasks – with the development of specific teaching competences associated with stimulating students' active engagement in their learning (Brouwer & Korthagen, 2005).

Interestingly, Burn and Mutton also outline that while there is good evidence from different contexts about the value of 'clinical practice', its impact is determined by the interplay between different components. Here we come back again to the findings of both Hammerness and Klette (2015) and Darling-Hammond et al. (2000) that quality teacher education is grounded in secure partnerships which are committed to making distinctive kinds of expertise and learning opportunities available to new teachers, but that also co-operate sufficiently closely to ensure genuine integration, leading to transformative teacher education experiences. Other approaches to teacher education which focus on research as pedagogy are discussed in Chapter 4.

The importance of values

So how can a teacher educator bring together a coherent programme with elements of core practices to develop certain high-leverage behaviours, and elements of research-based clinical practice, in a way that coalesces with various partners into a shared vision?

Rauschenberger, Adams and Kennedy's (2017) analysis of ways of measuring quality in teacher education illustrates how these elements can be combined to provide a quality experience. Through their analysis of approaches adopted in the United States, the Study of Effectiveness in Teacher Education (SETE) project from Australia and the TEDS-M cross-country study, they highlight that the values that underpin a programme can be significant drivers in ensuring consistency and context-sensitivity so that the elements of the programme hang together in a coherent way. Their work shows that different approaches are possible, and can yield high-quality results as long as they combine well and form part of an 'intelligent' evaluation framework (O'Neill, 2013). This aligns with the primacy of values for high-quality teacher education to underpin a coherent vision: without suggesting that those values need to be predetermined. They do need to be shared (with all partners and stakeholders), and they do need to permeate the programme design, curriculum and enactment, but this research also suggests that they need to sensitive to the context in which the teacher education occurs and to respond to that context.

What this chapter has argued therefore is that whilst the elements of a teacher education programme are pretty much the same in most contexts, it is the way that they are brought together and the values that unite them that can make the difference in quality (when we see quality as being about transformative educational experiences). How programmes are configured, and enacted reflects the values about teaching and teachers that underpin them. Programmes that are limited in scope or approach, either through overly zealous accountability or imposed constraints are unlikely to achieve that. Quality programmes may include a focus on core practices, and notions of partnership which recognize the contributions of experienced teachers and of research, but they also need to consider the individuals and the contexts. There is no magic bullet for quality teacher education; it appears to be a constant process of adjustment and becoming. Whilst research suggests a number of elements should be included, the quality of the experience will ultimately lie in their enactment.

As a final note for this chapter, I want to stress that it is the work of the teacher educators that bring these programmatic elements together (as we will explore in Chapter 5). They are the key actors who live out the values, strive for coherence across the programme, and seek to ensure that the opportunities to learn are meaningful. The judgement as to whether they have achieved this successfully will ultimately be determined if it gets the effects that the stakeholders consider valuable. And so, the next chapter explores the different ways in which that gets determined across various teacher education practices.

CHAPTER THREE

How Is Quality Teacher Education Determined?

Quality teacher education is a relative notion, which can be attributed to things which are hidden, which are difficult to define and even more difficult to judge. However, there are many attempts to pin down what quality in teacher education looks like, and different approaches used to make programmes accountable for how they reflect these definitions of quality. But does determining teacher education quality in this way work, and does the use of metrics play a role in making it more effective? Judgement in this sense is related to schemes of accountability, and teacher education can be an extremely highly regulated activity.

Judgements about quality in teacher education are often used to perform some sort of ranking function: to outline which programmes or providers are 'better' than others. To do this, judgements are based on data which are used as both measures and indicators of quality. The difference between the two is subtle: a measure might refer to a piece of data such as how many teachers graduate a programme, or how many successfully meet the relevant set of Teacher Standards. What can be measured is not always useful: the measure of the number of teacher graduates who are able to get jobs post-qualification is not a useful measure when there is a shortage of teachers, and nearly all who wish to become teachers can find gainful employment. The graduation rate or number of course completions is not a measure of the quality of the course but a measure of the number of people who successfully complete it. High graduation rates may indicate a course that is easy to pass or one where standards for graduation do not sufficiently differentiate competence.

An indicator is often related to a performance indicator, a threshold or benchmark of a particular measure. For example, in England, around 92 per cent of trainees on teacher education programmes successfully complete: if a programme has a score lower than this, then there is concern that there might be a quality problem with that programme. The benchmark of 92 per cent is an indicator.

Neither measures nor indicators are universally useful as markers of quality, as the element that is being measured does not necessary relate to the quality of the programme. Both measures and indicators require judgement in how they are interpreted. Such judgement needs to consider:

– What is being determined (whether the data refers to the individuals on the programme or the programme itself)

– For what purpose it is being determined (for example a programme with a low completion rate, may indicate very high standards of assessment, or poor levels of teaching, or inappropriate entry requirements).

In other words, the relationship between measures, indicators and the quality of a teacher education programme requires careful consideration. O'Neill (2013) differentiates between first-order tasks with second-order accountability measures. Accountability systems can confuse the proxy of second-order data with the quality of the first-order activity. When this happens, O'Neill suggests there are likely to be perverse outcomes. For example, the admissions system of a teacher education programme which is beholden of a performance indicator related to the number of students with a good degree from a recognized institution might exclude people who could potentially make good teachers but who do not meet this criterion. The criteria of prior attainment are not themselves a measure of quality of either the programme or the potential of someone to become a good teacher or who could teach well.

Similarly, Adams and McLennan (2021) note how judgements of quality (for initial teacher education) tend to be skewed towards the epistemological (knowledge and skills that can be displayed or seen) over the ontological (being, belonging and becoming a teacher). In other words, judgements around the quality of teacher education focus on what can be seen and what can be measured. Most of the measures and indicators that are used to determine quality in teacher education are indeed second order and epistemological: focusing on what can be measured and what can be seen but that does not reflect how teacher education can transform lay-people into new teachers: the real essence of quality in teacher education.

This is not to downplay the significant influence that such indicators can have. Indicators have become strong drivers influencing teacher education practices, and are at the centre of accountability policies around the world, as they make up an approach which Michael Barber (2007) described as 'deliverology': in that by collecting data on the right measure you can differentiate on quality and who is delivering on policy priorities. Accountability lays visible who is performing well, and who is performing less well but only against the indicators which have been set. The downsides of this approach have been widely reported as 'unintended harms' such as the widening of inequalities, forms of 'gaming the system' or outright cheating, a test-driven pedagogic culture and a narrowing of the curriculum (Gewirtz et al., 2019).

Ball and colleagues go further and argue that the discourse of 'standards'

> has the ability to arrange and rearrange, form and re-form, position and identify whatsoever and whomsoever exists

within its field and it has a 'heavy and fearsome materiality' …
This is a definitive move away from any attempt to create a
common or universal or comprehensive form of education
and towards (or back to) one which characterises, classifies
and specialises students distributed along a scale, around a
norm, in a system of infinitesimal disciplines which operates
on the 'under-side of law' as Foucault puts it.

(Ball et al., 2012, p. 514)

The impact of identifying particular measures or indicators
changes actions and practices. They also shift the discourse
about quality: focusing attention onto what is being measured
rather than whether the programme is being truly educational
or transformative. The problem with judging quality through
such indicators is that the underlying relationship between
that indicator and the intended outcome gets overlooked.

Quality, measures, standards and accountability

Teacher education is dominated by accountability regimes,
indicators, metrics and measures of quality (Bartell et al., 2018;
Sloat, Amrein-Beardsley, & Holloway, 2018; Watson, 2018).
Cochran-Smith and colleagues (2018) highlight the rise in
such metrics as part of the 'era of accountability' which they
attribute to five broad developments:

(1) unprecedented global attention to teacher quality, tied
to neoliberal economics;

(2) a continuous public narrative asserting that 'traditional'
university-sponsored teacher education was failing
to produce effective teachers who were prepared to
respond to the demands of contemporary classrooms;

(3) the conceptualization of teacher education as a public policy problem wherein it was assumed that getting the right policies in place would boost teacher quality and the national economy;

(4) the teacher education establishment's turn towards accountability, which was consistent with a conception of teacher quality defined as effectiveness and linked to the human capital paradigm; and

(5) the belief that the reform of public education, rather than other social policies, was the major tool for redressing inequality and eradicating poverty in the United States (Smith et al., 2018, p. 17).

Mayer (2017) notes that internationally the range of accountability measures introduced through policy developments is quite narrow, and Suzanne Wilson, in her lecture at AERA in 2018 made a list of all the quality measures she had encountered in teacher education, showing a narrow range of indicators each with similar features. Brooks (2021) categorized these quality indicators into four groups: measures that focused on processes, inputs, outputs and perspectives. I shall take each of these measures in turn and review what they tell us (and don't tell us) about quality teacher education.

Process indicators and measures

The processes of teacher education are the most challenging to define in terms of measures or indicators. Unlike other aspects of teacher education practice, processes do not lend themselves well to either items which can be measured or benchmark indicators. Where reviews have identified effective interventions, such as in the Hammerness and Klett (2015) research outlined in the previous chapter, they present opportunities to learn rather than quality processes in themselves.

However, there is a growing trend for policy interventions which seek to control or determine what happens in teacher education programmes. An example of this would be the suite of new measures introduced in England, which have received widespread political interest, and were referenced as good practice by the Next Steps report in Australia (Paul et al., 2021) (although erroneously credited as being introduced in the United Kingdom, rather than just being specific to England). The ITT (Initial Teacher Training) Core Content Framework in England needs to be seen as part of a wider suite of initiatives which seek to control teacher education practices, and that are a long way removed from encouraging quality in teacher education.

The ITT Market Review and Core Content Framework in England

The ITT Market Review was undertaken by an Expert Group convened by the Department of Education (DfE) of the British Government during 2020–21. The ITT Market Review applies only to teacher education (or initial teacher training [ITT] to use the DfE's vernacular) in England, as this responsibility is devolved to respective governments in Scotland, Wales and Northern Ireland. The review is a response to the highly differentiated landscape of teacher education (taught through a combination of university-led and school-based routes) that has emerged from previous policy initiatives, leading to a teacher education 'market' that is described as being both diverse and complex (Whiting et al., 2018).

The Market Review needs to be viewed as part of a suite of changes happening to teacher education. Ofsted, the government's inspectorate, had published a new ITT Inspection Framework focusing on judging the quality of curriculum (intent, implementation and impact) rather than outcome data, and a controversial and critical report into how teacher education providers had responded to the pandemic.

Teaching School Hubs, a major initiative in the teacher training infrastructure was announced, as was the national roll-out of a suite of government-owned professional development programmes (the Early Career Framework [ECF], and National Professional Qualifications [NPQs]), alongside the announcement that Teach First (a third sector organization linked with the Teach for All movement) has maintained their national contract with the DfE to train nearly 2000 teachers now for its nineteenth year. The tender process for a new government-initiated flagship teacher training institution, the Institute of Teaching, had also begun. In other words, the landscape of teacher education was changing and changing rapidly, with areas of content and delivery being centralized more and more to organizations directly controlled by the DfE. The stability of the 'market' was under threat.

The ITT Market Review group published their report in June 2021, which consisted of fourteen recommendations, and a list of Quality Requirements which would constitute the criteria for an accreditation process held for all new and current providers:

> The central aim of the review and our recommendations is to enable the provision of consistently high-quality training, in line with the CCF, in a more efficient and effective market.

The CCF referred to above is the government's ITT Core Content Framework (Department for Education, 2019) which 'defines in detail' the content of initial teacher training programmes as a 'minimum entitlement' which the DfE describes as drawing upon 'best available evidence' although this claim is disputed. The Market Review focuses heavily on 'evidence' (evidence is mentioned 88 times in the document, research: 40 times), which is taken from a range of government documents related to teacher education: the ITT Core Content Framework (CCF), the Early Career Framework and the national professional qualifications, each of which has been verified by the Education Endowment Foundation (the

CEO of which was on the Expert Group that authored the ECF and CCF).

The evidence cited in the Market Review document itself shows a preference for research generated outside of universities. The Market Review document contains citations of:

- four articles from peer-reviewed journals,

- four reports from non-university organizations, and

- eighteen government publications.

The dominance of research from non-university government-sponsored publications is indicative of the type of 'evidence' that is considered the preferred content for teacher education programmes.

The preference of evidence over research privileges a particular type of data gathering and 'what works' enquiries which have been widely criticized for their lack of contextual detail, ethical reflections and transferability (Biesta, 2007), and methodological robustness.

Whilst the ITT Market Review recommendations give primacy to the Core Content Framework as the required content for teacher education programmes, the publication of the document *Delivering World Class Teacher Development* by the DfE (2022) shows diagrammatically the relationship between the DfE, providers and other organizations in this new wave of policy (see Figure 3.1). Placing the DfE at the head of the diagram the document, the diagram is annotated as:

> The DfE created evidence informed frameworks, validated by the Education Endowment Foundation.
>
> (EEF)

In other words, this infrastructure places the DfE as the curator of what is considered appropriate research or evidence to be used as content for teacher education programmes. This goes a step further than previous reports which situate the teacher as

Annex B – Delivery infrastructure

1. The DfE created evidence informed frameworks, validated by the Education Endowment Foundation (EEF).

2. ECF and NPQ Lead Providers built on these frameworks to create evidence-informed curricula and establish national alliances of delivery partners.

3. From September 2022, the DfE will establish the Institute of Teaching, England's flagship teacher training and development provider.

4. Delivery partners will work with Lead Providers to deliver programmes across an area. Teaching School Hubs will be the backbone of these.

5. Schools choose their delivery partner and work with them.

6. Ofsted inspects Lead Providers and their delivery partners to drive up quality.

FIGURE 3.1 *ECF and NPQ delivery infrastructure (taken from* Delivering world-class teacher development, DfE, 2022*).*

a consumer of research (Carter, 2015), with teacher educators as the curators of that research, as it now places the DfE, and its affiliate organizations, as the authority who selects which evidence is appropriate for new teachers to learn.

Curating research and presenting it as content is of limited benefit for new teachers, as it renders them unable to consider practical implications of implementing research findings or the ability to judge the merits of research on its methodological rigour or contextual or situational appropriateness. In addition, the ITT Market Review recommendations outline the ways in which that content should be presented to new teachers through recommendations that stipulate how programmes should organize their assessment regimes, their practical learning experiences and their relationships with school partners and mentors. The recommendations outline the need for a specific, predetermined and pre-set 'sequenced curriculum' as a precondition for re-accreditation. The Core Content Framework defines the required content of teacher education programmes. The Quality Requirements laid out in the ITT

Market Review Recommendations defines the processes that are required for those programmes. The requirement for all teacher education programmes to go through an accreditation process ensures that all are aligned to both of the above. The determinants of quality of how teacher education programmes should be organized have effectively been entirely 'outsourced' to the government.

One of the Expert Group and chair of the CCF Expert Advisory Group, in a presentation at the Universities Council for the Education of Teachers conference in 2019, noted the significant content gaps in the CCF. There is widespread concern that the limited nature of the content, and the prescriptive nature of these proposals are aimed towards consistency (of content) in programmes and due to the prescriptive nature of the proposals are likely to reduce the opportunity for programme development to be achieved in collaboration with partners and that recognizes local need. Whilst introduced with the aim of improving the consistency of quality in teacher education, these proposals show a move to centralize control, prescribe content and restrict the opportunity for innovation in teacher education programmes: moves that are consistent with benchmarking processes, potentially to the detriment of transformative practices.

The trend of policies seeking to define or prescribe teacher education content can be seen in many forms elsewhere. The teacher education accreditation process in New Zealand required the inclusion of Key Tasks which needed to be reviewed by a panel of assessors. Whilst the long-term impact of these approaches is yet to be seen, it is potentially limiting to be prescribing the content of teacher education programmes, and outsourcing the expertise of teacher education provisions to government departments for education. Moreover, it is hard to imagine that this is actually a statement of quality teacher education: at best the prescription of content becomes a minimum baseline standard, a low bar, rather than a high one.

Input measures

A more popular group of measures of teacher education quality could be categorized as input measures. These are indicators that either look at the people who seek to become teachers and their characteristics (previous academic attainment, or graduation from an acceptable institution), or the qualifications and career trajectories of teacher educators. There are three noteworthy dimensions to this set of indicators. Firstly, this logic assumes that teacher education itself makes little impact on the quality of the teachers who graduate from it, but that the outcomes of a teacher education programme are driven, at least in part, by the people who sign up to it. In effect, quality in equals quality out: which begs the question of what difference the programme itself makes.

The second dimension is an assumption that 'high quality' applicants will make high-quality teachers. There is some evidence that so-called high-performing systems, as identified by international assessment comparison tests like PISA and TIMSS, have competitive entry requirements for new teachers, calling some to suggest that top graduates make 'good' teachers. However, there is no direct correlation between prior attainment and quality of teaching (Day, 2019; McNamara, Murray, & Phillips, 2017; Vagi, Pivovarova, & Barnard, 2019; Zhao, 2018; Zumwalt & Craig, 2005). It may also be the case that high-performing systems also enjoy higher status for teachers, or that there are other societal or economic factors which encourage some graduates to consider teaching.

The third dimension is the issue of defining what sort of qualities a high-potential or high-quality applicant to teacher education might look like. Frequently used, and readily available data measures include degree classification, or undergraduate institution. In other words, they tend to refer to pre-programme experience and prior educational achievement of the candidates. These characteristics do not directly correlate to the categories of either quality or standards around teaching, particularly as both of these characteristics are about academic achievement prior to pre-service preparation. Stobart (2008) argues that assessment is a form of sifting out people who can have access to scarcer and scarcer opportunities (entry to an elite institution, or achievement at a higher classification). In which case, other factors such as social class and cultural capital are more likely to be influential factors in gaining entrance to a programme with high entry requirements rather than the potential to be a good teacher. This would indicate that focusing on applicants with prior levels of high academic achievement could be seen as a way of restricting access to teaching to certain groups of potential applicants that may have high potential, and that may be more representative of the communities in which they will teach.

The idea that these characteristics of individuals are an indication of 'quality' in teachers or teaching is flawed but popular. Research that seeks to have a neat way of defining teacher quality often use it as a metric, for example Francis et al. (2019) use this as a metric of qualifications despite acknowledging its flaw as an indicator of teacher quality. As a benchmark, identification of prior education attainment is only an indicator of prior education attainment: not a predictor of teacher quality. If used as a way of judging the quality of a teacher education programme, then it could be an indicator of exceptionality, or exclusivity as more prestigious programmes with lower capacity are likely to be more challenging to gain access to. This is not an indicator of the quality of the programme, but might be related to the reputation of the institution.

Entrance characteristics used as indicators of quality are also silent on the issues around teacher supply and demand. Labaree (2006) notes how universities in the United States have struggled with the complexity of trying to raise the status of teacher education by increasing entry requirements, and then finding that local authorities (such as school districts) would introduce emergency certification for lesser-qualified teachers in order to meet the dip in teacher supply. He explains:

The need to produce a large number of teachers quickly meant that normal schools could not enforce an extensive and rigorous professional education. These schools operated under the constant threat of being by-passed. If they made access to or completion of teacher education very difficult, the number of graduates would decline and school districts would be forced to find other sources for teachers. One way or another, the classrooms would be filled, and the normal school leaders would fill them at whatever the cost.

(p. 24)

Labaree also notes a social mobility issue: teacher education is seen as the lowest status academic area with poor-quality research and low-status students (often women and those from disadvantaged groups). Indeed, for students, education is often seen as an entry profession for the socially mobile, those making the transition into the middle class and the first in their family to experience higher education (an observation supported by recent research from See & Gorard, 2019). Dissuading applicants of this nature to enter teacher education, through placing qualifications profile as an indicator of quality, suggests that programmes could be rejecting the very individuals for whom teacher education could be a pathway for social mobility, and who might be important representatives from marginalized communities.

In both New Zealand and Australia during the time of my research site visits in 2019 (Brooks, 2021), general employment markets were buoyant for new graduates. Students with a track record of good prior attainment (either at pre-graduate or graduate level) had a range of career options open to them. Similarly, the growth in university provision meant that students could pursue higher education in highly prestigious areas (like law or medicine) that may not have been previously accessible to them. As a result, the number of applicants for teacher education programmes dropped. The response to this was a reduction in entry requirements. Both in Queensland and Auckland, entry requirements for teacher education were significantly lower than the average university entry benchmarks. At the time of my data collection, neither location had an accountability regime which included input measures around graduate characteristics. However, the discourse of graduate quality was reflected in partnership-wide discussions about the 'calibre' of students, slipping standards and pre-service teachers' capacity for the classroom. In other words, the discourse itself, whilst not evident in the respective indicators, was having an impact on how the teacher education programmes were seen comparatively.

Input measures and diversity

Graduate diversity as an input measure does point to a different conception of teacher quality: one that suggests that representativeness of a diverse community is an important feature in the perceived quality of a teacher candidate. There is a growing body of evidence to suggest that teacher diversity can have a positive influence on student outcomes (Kumashiro, Neal, & Sleeter, 2015). Such positive influences can be seen for all students and not just those that share the teacher's cultural heritage. However, whilst promoting diversity in teacher applicants is an important objective, focusing on teacher diversity as a quality indicator for a teacher education programme does suggest that quality in teacher education is *determined* by the characteristics of teacher candidates (or applicants) rather than what happens during the process of being educated to be a teacher itself. In other words, this places the characteristic of the individual as the determining feature of teacher quality, rather than the process of teacher education that they go through.

This is not to suggest that an indicator on teacher diversity is not desirable, or indeed that a high-quality programme would not seek to diversify its intake. Focusing on diversity, whilst not a first-order factor in quality, would encourage providers to take positive steps to ensure a more diverse teacher workforce, which will have positive impacts on both students and schools. However, it is not in itself an indicator of the quality of the learning of that teacher education programme itself.

Output measures and perspectives

The most common measures used to determine teacher education quality are output measures, which can cover a range of outcome data such as completion rates, test scores, graduation and certification rates, employment rates, and a range of perspectival data stemming from graduates and new teachers, their employing schools, and even the perspectives of pupils and parents. There is also a growing range of indicators which use pupil performance data. To focus on outputs as a measure for quality assumes that the criteria being used such as the Teacher Standards are adequate and accurate descriptions of teacher (or teaching) quality; or that measures or tests of programme-based content knowledge correlate to high-quality teaching, or that only the best teachers are recruited into employment. They also assume that those factors are attributable to the programme itself (to the exclusion of other factors). However, these basic assumptions are deeply flawed as markers of quality teacher education.

In most contexts where meeting or evidencing the Teacher Standards is a prerequisite for qualification to become a teacher, the standards are a baseline description of teaching and incidences of failure to meet those standards are fairly low. In 2019, the Ofsted inspection framework in England shifted from a focus on output measures to one of curriculum quality. Under the previous inspection regime, providers had to produce a self-evaluation analysis of their output data against a set of national benchmarks. These included breakdown of employment rates, completion rates and the accurate 'grading' of teacher candidates. The Ofsted inspection framework clearly indicated that a provider could not be judged as Good or

Outstanding, unless their data exceeded national benchmarks. Consequently, it was highly unusual for any provider to report outcomes that were lower than those benchmarks. And as a result, around 98 per cent of providers were graded Good or Outstanding by Ofsted. Was this an indicator of high quality across teacher education providers, or that providers focused on meeting the benchmark target in terms of completion rates? Nevertheless, if nearly all the providers are demonstrating similar outcomes, then the indicator being used is no longer an indicator of quality, but becomes a baseline assessment or minimum expectation.

Other indicators such as those outside of the teacher education programme's control present their own problems. Using employment rates as an indicator of quality is severely compromised in times of teacher shortage, when the demand for teachers outstrips the supply. Even in times of a more selective employment market, it would not be accurate to assume that teachers are employed based on a rigorous analysis of the quality of their teaching or on how well they were prepared to teach. In addition, these metrics are short-term: employment, or assessment against a set of Standards relate to a specific point in time. They do not record the impact on teachers in the long term, and whether the teacher education programme prepared them to be classroom-ready or career-ready.

In other words, such outcome data is also second-order, reflecting other phenomena such as the employment market, rather than the quality of the programme itself. It is not surprising therefore, that there are also a range of indicators which have been developed which rely on the perspectives of new teachers (evaluating either their programme experience or their own teaching efficacy and competence), or from employers, partners or pupils. These indicators privilege stakeholders' views on quality, and whilst driven by a market-orientation to teacher education, have two main flaws in logic.

The first is where the customer, or student teacher, has a limited range of teacher education experiences upon which they can draw. Such perspectival information has reliability issues due to its accuracy and consistency (van der Lans, 2018). People are more likely to prefer that which is familiar, rather than the innovative or unusual. Respondents are also driven by self-interest (a good-quality course reflects well on those that have graduated from it). In addition, Gaertner and Brunner (2018) show that student perceptions of teaching quality are influenced by situational factors such as context and timing.

The second factor is that some school systems promote coherent identities (such as Multiple Academy Trusts in England, or Charter School chains in the United States) which feature strong narratives about quality; as such judgements of quality may be more driven by conformity and coherence to a prescribed set of values, then a more rounded, holistic (and even critical) notion of a quality teacher or quality teaching.

Perspectival data reveals what responders think is important, and whilst that might help determine differences between teacher education programmes, they are not in themselves reliable indicators of either quality or standards. However, indicators of this kind do have the potential of changing the relationship between the provider and stakeholders. Providers may be tempted to respond to requests in order to elicit positive feedback rather than to uphold challenging or uncomfortable aspects of a course which may be essential to its quality.

Finally, and probably more concerningly, there has been a recent growth in the measures which refer to the impact of student and newly qualified teachers on the progress and attainment of their pupils. These are referred to as value-added metrics. Despite the political attractiveness of this idea, it has been widely criticized for its lack of awareness of other factors to affect pupil attainment and simplistic linear logic, and validity (Noell, Burns, & Gansle, 2018; Sloat et al., 2018). The output indicators are more convincing however than the input indicators as they do have a (cause and effect) logic to them, even though they are mainly focused on standards rather than quality. Judgements based on output indicators need to be clear on what the indicators refer to.

So, what about Teacher Standards?

Measures become indicators when a benchmark performance is agreed as an indicator of success. In his discussion of quality in higher education, Harvey (2007) makes a distinction between indicators of quality and indicators of standards. He argues that quality can be defined in terms of something being exceptional, considered to be perfect or consistent in lacking imperfections, that it is considered fit for purpose, value for money or that it enables transformation to occur. He contrasts these definitions of quality with four types of standards, pointing out that in most higher education accountability systems the focus is on standards rather than quality. The four standards he identifies are academic standards, standards of competence, service standards and organizational standards.

Teacher education can be beholden to all of the above standards: it often has to be validated against a set of academic standards pertinent to the associated level of the academic award. Service and organizational standards are often related to student satisfaction surveys and requirements of service provision communicated to students prior to enrolment. Standards of competence however refer to the skills or behaviours that a graduate might expect such as Teacher Standards, and this category is often determined by groups outside of the higher education system: either government departments or professional bodies. Operating as a gatekeeper to the profession, Teacher Standards can influence the processes and the preferred outcomes of a teacher education course.

When an authority publishes a set of Teacher Standards, and a system by which new teachers are assessed and judged against them, they are in effect making a statement about society's baseline expectations of teachers. Therefore, how teacher standards are defined, and who defines them are important for shaping discourses around teacher education, and what quality in teacher education should look like. Analysis of teacher standards can therefore be very revealing as to the particular context of practice and the values and purposes that shape it.

Teacher Standards have also become ubiquitous around the world, and are often seen as a key policy initiative to affect the quality of teaching. Sachs (2003) has argued that they have significant potential to provide the necessary provocation for teachers to think about their work, classroom activities and professional identity in quite fundamental different and generative ways. When 'owned' by the profession, they can also offer great scope for professional autonomy and further professional learning. But teacher standards can also narrow teaching practice, reduce teacher autonomy and de-professionalize teachers (Bourke, Ryan, & Lidstone, 2012; Connell, 2009). Therefore, the questions of who owns and who defines the Teacher Standards are key in understanding the discourses of quality which underpin them, and the expectations that society has of its teachers.

This particularly struck me when I interrogated two sets of Teacher Standards: those of New Zealand, and Queensland, and compared them to the Teacher Standards I had been used to in England. New Zealand is a bi-cultural nation, which is reflected in the Teacher Standards, which embed the inclusion of Māori language, culture and knowledge, and consider its influences on educational practice. The policy documents which featured the revision of the Teacher Standards also referenced the motivation for New Zealand to improve in international comparisons, to focus on achievement, attainment and progress (as is the case in with many nations), but does so in a way that reflects a different set of values.

The language and tone of the New Zealand Code and Standards for Teachers (in 2017) is quite different to policy documents from other countries I have studied, both in the way that they pay homage to the profession and the consultation process, and in the specific recognition of Māori language and culture. This can be particularly seen in the expression of values that underpin the Teacher Standards, which are articulated not just in the Māori language but also through emphasizing Māori cultural perspective and priorities:

WHAKAMANA: empowering all learners to reach their highest potential by providing high-quality teaching and leadership.

MANAAKITANGA: creating a welcoming, caring and creative learning environment that treats everyone with respect and dignity.

PONO: showing integrity by acting in ways that are fair, honest, ethical and just.

WHANAUNGATANGA: engaging in positive and collaborative relationships with our learners, their families and whanau, our colleagues and the wider community.

The Code of Professional Responsibility echoes a commitment to Society, to the Teaching Profession, to Families and Whanau (a Māori term for extended family or community) and to learners: which is then broken down into a range of behaviours that go towards meeting that code. The Teacher Standards also reflect these perspectives, emphasizing Te Tiriti o Waitangi partnership, professional learning alongside professional relationships. The commitment to equity and Māori culture are reflected not just in the expression of the Teacher Standards but also in the resources made available to support the use of the standards for different teachers at different levels.

The Australian Teacher Standards are quite different not so much in their content and range but in how they were compiled and 'owned' by the Australian teacher's professional association. Within the Australian system, it is the Queensland College of Teachers which oversees and accredits teacher education provision for the state. Both the Standards and the Accreditation principles are influenced by the national Standards (*Australian Professional Standards for Teachers, APSTs*) and the Australian Institute for Teaching and School Leadership (AITSL) Accreditation of initial teacher education programmes in Australia Standards and Procedures. Clearly aligning both the Teacher Standards and the forms of accreditation with local and national professional bodies, had implications on how teacher education programmes were assessed and judged. During my research visit to Queensland, assessment of teacher candidates against the APSTs was placed as the sole responsibility of the school-based supervising teachers themselves. This was made possible because the APSTs were viewed as being 'owned' by the profession itself, and so the profession was trusted with their judicious application and the assessment of those standards. But this is not to say that the APSTs were popular: many teacher educators I spoke to agreed with Mockler (2013) that they were narrow in scope, and merely sought to standardize teachers' work, and with Sachs (2015) that they limited professional autonomy. (However, it is also noteworthy that the research was conducted at the start of the QTAP assessment initiative, one which has since proved to substantially change the landscape of the assessment of new teachers in the region, and in the involvement of university-based teacher educators in influencing how such assessments are made.)

Teacher Standards therefore are interesting tools that hold important messages about what is valued about teachers and teaching, who is trusted within the professional space to decide who should become a teacher, and the minimum levels of skills and behaviours they need to generate. As Evans (2008) notes, Teacher Standards are a performance management tool for controlling and influencing teachers' practice through the way in which it is described and compartmentalized. Evans refers to this as deduced or assumed professionalism which goes beyond prescription, as it articulates how professionalism is enacted by practitioners, and through doing so, makes that definition static.

Teacher education is also part of a wider landscape of accountability practices: including those pertaining to universities and to schools. This makes up a landscape of super-complexity (Ling, 2017) with multiple stakeholders, beholden to different accountability regimes. The role of accountability in defining quality within teacher education is significant: accountability regimes hold the power of accreditation, validation and, in the case of inspections, can award prestige in the field.

Accountability regimes may also affect how we think about teacher education through dominating the professional language used and limiting those that hold and retain power to influence how these policy documents are written (and what is omitted). Teacher Standards do this in two ways: by influencing the language of teacher education: how progress, achievement and attainment are expressed; and also, by setting a minimum benchmark bar for how teaching competence is judged. In some accountability regimes that focus on outputs, completion and attainment rates (how many people pass and meet the standards) are used as a benchmark for programme quality. This presumes and presupposes that Teacher Standards are a sufficient differentiator between people who can teach well and those who can't. However, once Teacher Standards have been established they become the lowest denominator and all courses adapt for maximum completion rates. When accountability measures are introduced they then become the benchmark which becomes the focus for what teacher education is seeking to achieve and so closes down discussion, innovation, debate and alternative viewpoints. As Sleeter (2019) argues, such definitions of quality sustain the status quo of who holds power and who is able to define quality.

Accountability mechanisms like Teacher Standards can have the effect of instrumentalizing practice: to parse it down so that it can be rebuilt in the novice incrementally, and ticked off once it has been achieved. This is not the language or practice of transformation. But it is the reality of teacher education today in many countries. It is not the case that accountability necessarily takes away criticality or transformation, but it can reduce the opportunity for it to occur productively, and so could have the effect of reducing teacher education to replication rather than transformation.

CHAPTER FOUR

Can Alternative Approaches Improve the Quality of Teacher Education?

So far, different perspectives on quality have been treated rather critically, arguing that the relationship with quality (when understood as transformation) is rather limited. This chapter focuses on initiatives that have been introduced in order to improve the quality of teacher education. Journals are full of evaluative accounts of initiatives that have sought to make improvements to the experience of learning to teach: often through focusing on improving mentoring, partnerships or creating stronger links between theory and practice. Many of these accounts are based on interventions that are small scale and are highly context specific (Menter, 2017), and so may not have wider applicability for larger-scale quality interventions. This chapter will therefore focus on two system-wide approaches with the stated intention of improving teacher education quality: through diversifying the range of teacher education providers or through emphasizing research as a dominant approach to improving and professionalizing teaching.

Alternative provision

Chapter 1 outlined how universities are often seen as the source of the quality 'problem' in teacher education, through being overly abstract and removed from the classroom. It is not surprising therefore, that some policy initiatives have called for a diversification of providers of teacher education and greater involvement of schools in the design of teacher education programmes. An extreme example would be the highly diversified school-led teacher education system in England through the introduction of a school-led route known as School Direct (Brown, 2017; Tatto, Burn, Menter, Mutton, & Thompson, 2017). Whilst attributed by some to political motives rather than a genuine concern for teacher education quality (Ellis, 2019; Ellis & Spendlove, 2020), the resulting landscape of teacher education is highly diversified and complex (Whiting et al., 2018), and about to be changed due to the policy shifts and the market review outlined in Chapter 3.

A shift of different sorts has been experienced in the United States, through the growth of alternative provision schemes such as the new Graduate Schools of Education (nGSEs). Cochran-Smith and colleagues (Cochran-Smith, 2020; Cochran-Smith et al., 2020) define the nGSEs as 'not university based, but are state authorized and approved as institutions of higher education to prepare teachers, endorse them for initial teacher certification, and grant master's degrees' (Cochran-Smith et al., 2020, p. 9). They argue that these are a distinct group of teacher education providers because they are not part of the tradition and culture of universities but still rely on their symbolic indicators of professional legitimacy and access. Attributing the growth of nGSEs to the conception of teacher education as a policy problem in the United States, nGSEs were seen as a way of providing an alternative to teacher education provision that would be freed from some of the perceived restraints of university-based provision.

Established in the last two decades, nGSEs are either independent stand-alone institutions or part of larger non-university entities, which are authorized to grant masters degrees and are accredited institutionally and programmatically to provide initial-level teacher preparation. The nGSEs often use the academic nomenclature of universities (e.g. graduate school of education, graduate school, teachers college, dean, academy). Cochran-Smith et al. (2020) suggest that an important feature of teacher preparation at nGSEs is the operating assumption that teaching is a learned activity that builds on, but goes beyond, individuals' subject matter knowledge, motivation, and/or aptitude. nGSEs are likely to use terms such as internship, apprenticeship or residency to describe their programmes although these terms are not limited to nGSEs.

As part of a Spencer Foundation-funded project to review the nGSEs, Cochran-Smith and colleagues highlight that there is considerable variation between them. But they do provide an incredible opportunity to think about teacher education differently, and to provide innovative ways of diversifying ways of becoming a teacher, for example through employment-based or online/digital formats. This is not to suggest that university providers are not innovative (e.g. see the account of the Mary Lou Fulton Teachers College's Next Education Workforce initiative referred to in Chapter 5), but they are often constrained by structures, university regulations and other requirements that prevent them from wholesale rethinking how teacher education can be organized.

Perhaps unsurprisingly, alternative provision has been met with suspicion and criticism from teacher educators. However, nGSEs should not be considered an homogeneous group: as Cochran-Smith argues it has been 'demonstrated repeatedly in empirical studies and argued in policy reports, there was often as much variation *within* "new" approaches as there was *between* "new" and "traditional" approaches, accompanied by inconsistencies in terminology that made valid comparisons nearly impossible'. But they have been widely criticized for their approaches to professional learning, how they conceptualize teaching, and their overall quality (Philip et al., 2018; Schorr, 2013; B. A. Smith, 2015; Stitzlein & West, 2014; Zeichner, 2016). However, the opportunity to explore innovative practices of these alternative providers may be hindered by the ways in which they are set up as competitors to more traditional teacher education programmes, supported by additional funding models (such as from venture philanthropists) which are not available to traditional university-based provision.

It could be argued that a major opportunity for nGSEs, particularly as they are freed from the confines of university admission procedures, is that they can open up the possibility of teacher education for under-represented groups. The desire to broaden the groups of individuals who might wish to become teachers, particularly to diverse groups who may not initially perceive teaching as a career choice. This may be due to perceptions of teaching as a white, middle-class profession, reflected in a number of barriers to entry which might include the entry requirements of traditional teacher education programmes which necessitate a tradition or 'standard' academic history of success, and the training programme arrangements which require candidates to take a year of unpaid (and sometimes costly) studies incurring debt and loss of income. This is quite different to the approach of the Teach for All movement (or Teach First) which tends to focus on attracting high academic attainers, rather than those from marginalized or under-represented groups.

For example, Caperton and Whitmire (2012) noted how some nGSEs have sought to reinvent how teachers are prepared for high-need urban schools. In 2016/17 the website for the Relay Graduate School of Education stated that 70 per cent of Relay residents identified as Black, Latino or Asian. The website also promoted the kinds of communities described as 'underserved' and 'deserving' that are targeted by the Relay Graduate School of Education.

The need to diversify the population attracted into teaching is great particularly from under-represented groups. However, if there are doubts about the quality of the teacher education experience then programmes that focus on diverse groups may be doing more damage than good, particularly if they are seen as being of less quality, having a limited repertoire and cover a limited range of (core) teaching practices and denying new teachers access to potentially transformative theoretical knowledge (Philip et al., 2018). Indeed it has also been suggested that they are based on deficit models that circumscribe students' possibilities (B. A. Smith, 2015). In other words, if the programmes that are specifically targeted at low-income schools and marginalized communities are not offering high-quality teacher education then they may reproduce those inequalities and prevent those involved from critiquing the power dynamics that have caused them.

Whilst the nGSEs do provide an opportunity to view teacher education in different ways, their impact and quality remains unclear. It is also important that they are not seen as the only innovative programmes within teacher education. Other potential disrupters in the field include online programmes at NYU Steinhardt, Auckland's Teaching for Equity and the Clinical Practice model in Melbourne, and the MSc in Transformative Learning and Teaching based in Edinburgh. These programmes also seek to consider other ways of thinking about high-quality programme provision, often reflecting individualized or small group inquiries, individual reflection and research, and situated personal mentoring and coaching. These approaches are focused on the individual teacher-in-training (sometimes also referred to as residency), and offer a highly personalized pathway to competence, achieved through what they describe as high-quality, high-engagement partnerships where school-based mentors work with the new teachers and support their individual development. These approaches are expensive, but not limited to the nature of the teacher education provider.

As a final word, having looked at Teach for America as an example of alternative provision, Ing and Loeb's (2008) research suggests that the variability in quality of teacher education programmes is not hugely different from other providers. Indeed, the basic characteristics of teacher education appear to be applied across both traditional and alternative programmes: suggesting a hegemony around teacher education pedagogies. They argue that it is the capacity of a programme to adapt to individual needs of teachers, and the particular contexts of schools that marks out whether a programme can be considered high quality or not.

Policy orientation towards research

In Chapter 2, I outlined reviews of clinical practice as an effective approach to teacher education. One of the elements of clinical practice is its proximity to research or inquiry as a form of teacher preparation and indeed as a desirable feature of teacher professionalism. There are few examples however of education policy which foregrounds research within teacher education, despite consensus within the academic community that this should be a desirable feature. The two approaches discussed below (from Norway and Wales) show how such an approach needs to understand the ways in which teacher education sits within the wider educational infrastructure, and what lessons can be learnt from experienced research-orientated programmes such as the one from OISE in Toronto.

The Welsh National Strategy for Education Research and Enquiry

Developed in response to disappointing educational performance in Wales, the Welsh government announced a new vision for teacher professionalism, articulated in their National Strategy document, published in June 2021. The Aim of the Strategy foregrounded research in all aspects of educational policy and practice:

The aim of the NSERE is that educational policy and practice in Wales should be informed by the best available research evidence and disciplined enquiry undertaken by educational professionals.

The specific strategy objectives recognized that this needed to be achieved through a research orientation in all aspects of the education system: from policy making, the development of research capacity and volume, through to how educators interacted with that research evidence, and the infrastructure that was needed to sustain it. The Welsh National Strategy, as Furlong (2019) outlines, has to be seen as part of an integrated education strategy in Wales designed to improve the quality of education provision and teacher professionalism that also includes teacher-led school and curriculum reform.

The National Strategy makes an important distinction between the different roles and functions of research in initial teacher education highlighting the difference between research and enquiry but committing to both:

> We recognise that 'research' can encompass a spectrum of activities that utilise research methods. We do not subscribe to a view that research is something that can only be done by professional educational researchers and not by educational professionals. We are interested in the concept of a 'continuum' of development whereby educational professionals move from being professional enquirers to becoming teacher researchers.

The National Strategy also supports the idea of teachers as both consumers and producers of research:

> The developments we propose to undertake will focus on enabling practitioners to be both consumers of high-quality research and producers of professional enquiry that is informed by rigorous research methods. This is the reason why we choose to have both 'research' and 'enquiry'

included in our strategy, so that the approach we take in Wales is inclusive and 'close to practice'.

Acknowledging the difference between research and enquiry, the Strategy emphasizes that they are 'of equal value and interdependent':

- 'Academic research' is a process of investigation leading to new knowledge. It is published so that others can learn from and critique it. To be regarded of high quality it should be significant, original and rigorous. To that end, it should be peer-reviewed before it is published. This type of research is usually undertaken by academics, those studying for higher degrees and professional researchers working in the government and independent sectors.

- 'Professional enquiry' is usually undertaken by practitioners within their workplace as a way of identifying problems, establishing causes, finding solutions, evaluating practice and achieving improvement. If it is to be of value it should utilize action research approaches that are systematic, cyclical and that emphasize the collection of evidence.

Such a nuanced understanding is also reflected in the recognition and commitment to enhancing the research capacity of universities, through building on the current research structures, but also by raising expectations on teacher educators and their active involvement in research. Gaps in the current provision and capacity are noted and pledges made for the support needed to bridge the gap between vision and reality of the research capacity for teacher educators.

The National Strategy builds on the new Accreditation Criteria (established in 2017) which outlines an approach to teacher education which Furlong (2019) describes as 'research informed clinical practice' (after Burn & Mutton, 2013) which is different to 'research-informed' practice, professional learning based on trial and error, or reflection based on experience. It requires schools as well as universities to provide the opportunities for research-based professional learning. Reviews of the progress of this strategy indicate that it is still in the early stages but is potentially transformative (Brooks, 2022).

Transformational change in Norway

In 2013, Karen Hammerness published a review of teacher education programmes in Norway, in relation to the three key features of powerful education programmes identified by Darling-Hammond and colleagues (Darling-Hammond, 2006; Darling-Hammond & Berry, 1999) (vision, coherence and opportunities to learn that are grounded in teaching practice). Her review was critical: suggesting that teacher education programmes lacked a shared vision, and have few opportunities for student teachers to learn in a context of practice. It was not surprising then, that Hammerness became part of the International Advisory panel for Primary and Lower Secondary Teacher Education, whose proposals on Transforming Norwegian Teacher Education promote a strong emphasis on research.

Success of any initiative depends on what it was seeking to achieve, and how it defines the expectations around quality. The recommendations contained within Transforming Norwegian Teacher Education were directed both at the Ministry of Education and its constituent groups, and at Teacher Education Institutions. For the Ministry of Education, the focus was on changing the accountability system to focus on responsibility, agency and innovation rather than monitoring compliance and uniformity, and the implications this would have on sustainability, funding and supporting effective partnerships. For the Teacher Education Institutions and schools, the recommendations focused on building research capacity, developing a research-based approach to programme design and integration, and in the development of partnerships and school experience. It also included recommendations about how this partnership would best mutually support masters-level work in teacher education.

What both the Norwegian review recommendations and the Welsh Strategy have in common is a recognition of the primacy of research as a key driver for quality educational experiences, and the need for investment to support a research infrastructure. The need for this investment in research is universal, as reviews emphasize that research in teacher education is often partial, limited and narrow in scope. Although the impact of these reforms in Wales and Norway have yet to show their impact, they both take an alternative view not just of how quality in teacher education might look like (with an emphasis on research and strong university–school partnerships). The proposals also see a research-orientation as a way of creating sustainable and systemic change that is in contrast to accountability and compliance policies often used elsewhere. In effect, they are investing in research as a mechanism to professionalize and inform teaching, which will in turn have an impact on quality.

In my discussions with a teacher educator in Wales, there was a recognition that the implementation of the Strategy was experiencing challenges: such as the opportunity (as well as capacity) for teacher educators to become fully research-active, and for new teachers and schools to understand the role and opportunities that research offers them. Whilst there has been an evidential shift in the expectations of new teachers as they graduated through the teacher education programmes, the transition to a more 'researcherly disposition' was a challenge. An advantage of the Welsh strategy is the clear distinction it makes between research and enquiry: a distinction that teacher educators who have been engaged in research-based approaches for some time are still finding challenging.

Research-orientated teacher education at OISE

The Ontario Institute for Studies in Education (OISE), an institution recognized for its innovative research into education based at the University of Toronto, runs a Master of Teaching programme, the only graduate-level entry teacher education programme in Ontario, and along with McGill University in Quebec, one of only two across Canada (Baxan & Broad, 2017). A key feature of this teacher education programme is its grounding in research both in content, pedagogy and practice, as shown in how it is given equal weight in the programme structure with the Academic Program and the Practice Teaching elements. This is clear in the programme's vision:

> Teaching excellence and scholarly research are the mutually reinforcing pillars of the Master of Teaching program. The program prepares candidates to become outstanding teachers and leaders who consult, critique, create and mobilize educational research. … Research is at the core of the Master of Teaching degree program. A unique aspect of your experience as an MT student is that you have course-based opportunities to learn about educational research methodologies, to conduct research in an area of specialization that interests you, and to produce graduate level scholarship.
>
> (MT Programme Handbook, 2020)

Research in embedded in the academic courses that teacher candidates are required to take and the assessment of an original research paper, and conference presentation. Research in intended to be part of what the new teachers learn (the ability to situate research as a way of both informing and developing practice, but also recognizing its situation within the field) but is also the dominant pedagogy of learning to teach: 'Findings from your research will inform your own teaching practice and professional identity as teacher-researchers' (MT Programme handbook).

This approach does present problems for the programme though. OISE has had to consider the research capacity of the staff teaching on the programme, many of whom are 'sessional' staff: part-time lecturers who teach and supervise on the programme, and some of whom may hold similar positions elsewhere. Whilst these staff members may hold doctorates in relevant fields, the OISE team have developed professional development initiatives (to share research outcomes and approaches amongst the teaching team) and research-funding streams to support these colleagues to maintain their active engagement in research. This is based on their belief that for a research-orientated programme, it is important for the staff teaching on that programme to be research active themselves. As a result, there appears to be strong coherence about the role and value of research across the teaching team.

In addition, as research has become more and more embedded in the programme, questions have arisen as to how it relates to the development of teaching skills and behaviours, the participation and involvement of school partners, and the sorts of research methodologies that new teachers need to understand. The programme leadership continue to question and review the role of research on the programme.

> It's one of the key questions, I think. So, what does a research informed teacher education program or research at graduate level teaching program look like? How has the emphasis shifted? I think of how we assess students, and that most of them would see the research as isolated. So, it's a research-intensive program, but the big question we were moving to is what does it mean to be masterly? What makes this program at a master's level?
>
> (OISE, Interview, 2020)

Such reflections and questions are insightful, particularly in the light of the move to a more research orientation as a way of improving quality in teacher education provision. They reflect questions about the relationship between research and learning to teach, the infrastructure that is necessary for that and the demands it can place on teacher educators.

An approach to teacher education that focuses on the outcome indicators outlined in Chapter 3, and teacher behaviours outlined in Chapter 2, can be limited in scope. A more research-orientated approach opens up possibilities for a teacher education that reflects a broader conceptualization of the behaviours, skills and the knowledge and understanding needed for situational judgement: a key feature of teaching as a profession. Adopting a research perspective could enable a form of professional learning that emphasizes options and flexibility; in other words that has adaptivity at its core. Menter and colleagues (2010) show how different emphasizes in teacher education can position research differently: for example, a focus on

- The effective teacher: with an emphasis on meeting standards and competences, positions research as content to be digested and understood;

- The reflective teacher: with an emphasis on individual professional development achieved through practice positions research as being a tool with which to challenge assumptions based on experience;

- The enquiring teacher: adopts an enquiry approach, which in some cases has veered towards a research orientation;

- The transformative teacher: who adopts an activist stance in relation to enquiries in order to contribute to social change, and sees research as emancipatory.

Research can therefore be seen as a way of challenging assumptions about teaching, as a way of investigating and inquiring into practice that reflects local contexts, needs and discourses about teaching, but also as a way of challenging issues of equity, and justice that exist within education, and therefore can provide a range of ideas possible for a teacher education that enables transformation.

CHAPTER FIVE

Adapting for Quality Teacher Education

Perspectives on quality in teacher education can vary, and are largely dependent on the focus of what is being valued. Official definitions of quality, articulated through Teacher Standards, accountability measures, and even the results from research can be distant to the day-to-day practices of teacher educators. This chapter explores how teacher educators have adapted their practice in order to enact what they understand to be quality teacher education. This account of quality as transformation is probably the closest to the experiences of new teachers. It is highly contextual and deeply rooted in its location, and shows what can be done to enhance quality in otherwise-restrictive contexts. These accounts reflect how quality teacher education often has to work around the unique arrangements of accountability, structures, partnership and availability of students in each location, and as such it focuses on the work of teacher educators and contrasts with other initiatives that have been developed by policy or government initiatives.

In my research, conducted in 2018–20, I observed five teacher education programmes in five different international contexts (Brooks, 2021). During my site visits I talked to a range of teacher educators, observed their practice and

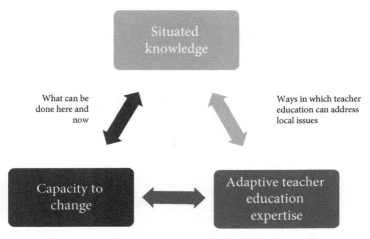

FIGURE 5.1 *Model of teacher education practice.*

collated examples of them working in different contexts with very different pressures. In response, I saw people working highly adaptively, and represented this in my model of teacher education practice illustrated above (see Figure 5.1).

The model of teacher education practice was developed through empirical data analysis and was verified and discussed with key actors, participants and stakeholders in each of the locations of the research. It reflects three areas of knowledge which I have called spatial knowledges because they are firmly located in the site (or location) of each of the programmes I researched. The layout of the model is arranged to show how these spatial knowledges are related and interconnected, but in particular how the adaptivity of the work of teacher educators brings together the contexts in relation to what is possible and what is desirable. The relationships in the model are also bi-directional: spatial influences will affect practices and pedagogy and in turn these may shape ways of knowing about teacher education. The framework is designed as a way of laying these elements out, showing how they intersect and inter-relate.

Teacher educators undertake their work within a range of influences, parameters, accountability measures and opportunities. The model attempts to capture these opportunities and how they influence the practice of teacher education.

- **Situated knowledge:** Teacher educators have an in-depth knowledge of education in both a broad and localized sense: they draw upon a detailed understanding of the catchment area of their programme, its unique features and key issues/priorities. This understanding is situated within national and global discourses: so that they are able to understand, for example, how the specific demand for new teachers in their local area reflects national trends and initiatives pertinent to teacher recruitment. They are also aware of the individuals who are involved: who chooses to become a teacher here, who will they be working with, and what do the local schools need and want? The localized knowledge is highly situational: it includes educational debates and issues, but views them specifically in relation to how they are played out locally. One would anticipate that within a teacher education programme located in higher education settings this knowledge would also be informed by the research literature. The knowledge is dynamic and will be affected by trends in education that affect schools, as well as new research findings related to teacher education.

- **Adaptive teacher education expertise:** Teacher education is situated within complex accountability structures and multiple stakeholders across a range of organizations including universities and schools, and how this can influence pedagogy and practice. Teacher education expertise therefore stems from a range of sources including theories of professional learning, the experience of working with new teachers in a range of contexts, and knowledges of learning and teaching from other fields and from research. This specialist teacher education expertise is grown from, but distinct to, the experience of teaching, and has to be highly adaptive to local and dynamic contexts, as well as new findings from research. This knowledge base enables teacher educators to make informed decisions about how to structure, teach and assess their programmes, and when used adaptively includes a range of innovative possibilities that could be used flexibly within teacher education.

- **Capacity to change:** The ability to make decisions about practice and pedagogy can be limited and constrained by factors within a particular context such as university governance systems, local funding or accountability arrangements, or practice traditions around partnership. Universities and schools are necessarily designed for other activities (such as research, teaching and education of students or pupils), and so their systems may not be optimum for teacher education. Therefore, any adaptations that teacher educators wish to make need to be adjusted with these constraints (and opportunities) in mind. (taken from Brooks, 2021, pp. 204–5)

In the five teacher education programmes that I studied, I saw examples of teacher educators working adaptively, in and around the sorts of knowledges and capacities that I have described above. Each context was unique, and so the individual actions were different.

In Arizona, where there was a chronic need for new teachers particularly in some school districts, the development of the Next Education Workforce initiative was introduced by the Mary Lou Fulton Teachers College based at Arizona State University, so that school districts could employ teacher candidates in the final year of their education programme, to work in teams under the supervision of a lead teacher. This provided a dual function in enabling teacher candidates to get some payment for the final year of their studies alongside their necessary practicum experience, as well as going some way to supporting the teacher supply issue. Moreover, by being employed by the School Districts, it was hoped that this would encourage the teacher candidates to continue their careers post-qualification in the very areas where demand for teachers was high. This innovative approach was also grounded in an understanding of the complexity of teaching, and the importance of developing a community of practice to support new teachers.

In terms of the teacher education experience, this approach required a number of necessary changes. As the lead teacher, the school-based mentor had responsibility for a team of student teachers (three) for an entire academic year, along with the shared responsibility of two classes (their own and that allocated to the team of student teachers). The process of mentoring changed during the duration of that year, but also depending on the various needs of the particular student teachers. In addition, the site lead, who had oversight of the mentors and teachers within her area, also had changed her role. The new arrangements allowed her to spend more time in class with the teacher candidates and this was positively affecting the mentoring support she could offer. Although the site lead was considerably more experienced (both as an educator and as a teacher educator) than the lead teacher, they both recounted in-programme adaption to their teacher education work: adaption that appeared to complement each other's changing roles, and that were responsive to the ebb and flow of the school year, the differing needs of the three student teachers, and the specific needs of the class they were working with. The developmental nature of the programme meant that they were given a lot of capacity to make these changes in-year and to use this experience to feedback to the programme team to inform further developments.

The role of the lead teacher was a key professional development opportunity for the school-based teacher. As the leader of the team, she was now responsible for three teacher candidates and sixty students and had all the associated responsibility for planning, assessment, welfare and family liaison. In addition, the lead teacher is also a colleague of the teacher candidates, and had to oscillate between being mentor, colleague and guide. These new roles provide the lead teacher with valuable professional development particularly around leadership skills, but they also require a different skill set to the role of mentoring alone. There is a shift in the balance of those roles over time: the lead teacher described modelling more at the beginning of the year, and as the new teachers developed, moving into a more collaborative approach working alongside them.

Similarly, the site lead discussed how her role had shifted to one that was more of a 'team member', working with the lead teacher as well as with the taking on some of the mentoring of the teacher candidates. The site lead still held responsibility for the completion of lesson observation paperwork and other assessment documentation, but the role had become more akin with mentoring, and working on the individual development of the teacher candidates. As someone with extensive previous experience as a mentor, she was comfortable with this shift in roles, and described drawing on her extensive mentoring experience to enable her to move between these roles as needed, and to support the lead teacher as her role changed. Both the school-based and university-based teacher educators showed high levels of adaptivity, responding to changes happening throughout the school year, and in relation to the changing needs of the student teachers required by the change in programme structure.

One further area that was in the process of review was in how the taught courses (in the three years of the programme prior to the final year practicum experience) also required adaptation. These colleagues, described locally as academic faculty, were also finding that their roles were shifting and reforming. As the implications of a practicum experience at the end of the programme were being understood, so they were considering what adaptations needed to be made to the curriculum, although at the time of the research this was still in the early stages.

The notion of adaptivity outlined above presupposes that teacher educators have the agency and capacity to adapt their practice. This was the case in the Next Education Workforce initiative, but is not always possible. Changes to teacher education programmes can be imposed externally, without the necessary flexibility for adaptation. The teacher education programmes at the IOE (Institute of Education, University College London) were constructed around a spiral curriculum model, similar to that described by Biesta (2019). On the Primary programme this was described as a process of learning loops, so that through the three blocks of school experience, the main strands of learning to teach were reviewed in the light of the student teachers' growing experience and expertise. This process however, was interrupted by a government mandate about the teaching of phonics, which required that most of the phonics teaching was scheduled at the start of the programme. The teacher educators were unhappy with this approach, as they felt the phonics content and the student teacher's classroom experiences were misaligned, meaning that the student teachers were unable to make the most of linking theory and practice. Whilst this illustrates the limitations in the capacity to change, the teacher educators drew upon their situated knowledge (of how their partner schools taught phonics), and their own adaptive practice to ensure that this learning was consolidated later in the programme, both through the expectations around the school-based experiences and in the content and approach of the university taught sessions. In other words, a policy initiative that was a potential barrier to quality was worked around through the adaptivity of the teacher educators.

This tension between differing perspectives on quality is commonplace, even when all partners are united in the vision for what a programme should achieve. The University of Edinburgh's MSc in Transformative Learning and Teaching, referred to in Chapter 1, is an example of a programme that has been specifically designed around the idea of transformation and the development of an activist teaching profession (Sachs,

2003). The programme was designed to support this vision through three distinctive elements:

- Masters-level engagement to support a critical, activist orientation to teaching;

- An assessment philosophy that sees all assessment activities as being professionally authentic, sustainable, collaborative and student-driven; and

- A focus on site-based learning as fully integrated into the programme (Kennedy, 2018).

Despite the opportunity to build such a programme, with the key features of having a shared vision, coherence and due attention to the opportunities to learn (as discussed in Chapter 2), Kennedy outlines that there were still significant counter narratives across three distinctive cultural spaces (the political, professional and university). In the case of the above programme, Kennedy outlines the adaptivity required to work through these narratives. And as with the IOE programme, the focus of the adaptivity generally lies with the teacher educators. This is significant when the potential barriers to quality are located outside of their scope of influence, and does pose questions about what can be done about the more systemic threats to quality.

Not all barriers to quality are initiated by government mandates. In the research, I learnt of a number of incidences of teacher educators having to work around university-orientated or school-based structures that were less than optimum for the teacher education experience. For example:

- Changes in the arrangements of the payment for mentor teachers affected who could be mentors for new teachers;

- University workload and timetabling policies prevented innovative practices bringing together student teachers, mentors and university tutors at key points throughout the academic year;

- Academic year structures dominated when assessments could happen or when practicums could take place, making explicit links between theory and practice challenging;

- University faculty recruitment policies prevented some highly skilled and experienced teachers from joining the programmes as faculty members;

- Promotion frameworks disadvantaged teacher educators who lacked a traditional research-orientated career-trajectory, or who invested in relationship and partnership management for the benefit of the teacher education programmes.

In each of the examples given above, teacher educators recounted working adaptively in a way that often prioritized the experience of their student teachers, over their own careers. Teacher educators worked hard to develop and support new mentors, to undertake teaching without it counting as part of their workload, or described operating flexible teaching schemas and working beyond module schedules, or foregoing promotion opportunities to focus on providing quality teacher education experiences. In these examples, and I am sure in others, it was the commitment of these teacher educators that ensured that new teachers on their programmes had quality transformative experiences.

However, whilst it is a pleasure to outline accounts of teacher educators doing quality work, it is important to recognize the limitations and costs of doing so. Central to the maintenance of high-quality teacher education practices is the adaptive expertise of teacher educators, which necessarily varies across different locations and roles (particularly between university, schools and other partners). It is necessary in both leaders and individual teacher educators. Approaches which are too fixed or dogmatic are unlikely to respond to a changing local context. Teacher educators themselves often fail to recognize this expertise, or to appreciate its adaptive nature when responding to dynamic definitions of quality or local changes in practice (and indeed not all teacher educators are able to work so adaptively, or have the necessary expertise needed). Adaptive teacher education expertise is particularly important in a context where many university-based teacher educators are employed on temporary, casual, and teaching-only contracts.

However, accountability, judgements and arrangements around teacher education, which can influence how it plays out, are not always focused on what really influences quality in education, but can direct attention to proxies for quality. These can have what O'Neill (2013) described as perverse effects. Systems with a limited capacity for change, for example, in a highly regulated context with a prescriptive curriculum, will likely restrict opportunities for innovation, or adaptations. High-stakes accountability systems will draw attention to that which is measured rather than the practices that can lead to transformation. The capacity to change may be outside of the scope of the teacher educators, or indeed the university's Education department or faculty. It may be controlled externally by professional associations or government bodies. It may also be contingent on individual institutions, through the autonomy and agency afforded to individual teacher educators or programme leaders. There is a need then for what O'Neill has described as 'intelligent accountability' that where there is a clear distinction between what is being measured, and what is being judged, and there is a recognition that practices that may lead to transformation are incredibly difficult to measure.

The importance of partnerships

One of the drawbacks of the model of teacher education practice is that it could be read as a highly individualized way of considering quality. Partnerships are central to the work of teacher education. Teacher educators need to ensure that schools and universities work together in the best possible way. Much of the literature argues for a less hierarchical partnership arrangement, recognizing schools as more than a site of practice, but as an equal partner in the provision of teacher education. However, the reality is more challenging. Educational institutions are hierarchical by nature (Labaree, 2006), and there is a tension between the hierarchy of the academic work of universities and the practice of teaching which happens in schools. It is not surprising then, that the teacher education literature emphasize that partnership should be collaborative, but as Smith, Brisard and Menter (2007) suggest, most teacher education partnerships are not of this nature, as there are a number of barriers to the formation of such partnerships.

Partnership formations are made possible through different funding models, and levels of expectations for involvement afforded directly to schools. In the case of schools in Queensland, and the Normal Schools in New Zealand, schools have a vested interest in being involved in teacher education, and are remunerated directly for it, or held to account through their periodic review. In Arizona, involvement in teacher education was seen as a key strategy to ensure future teachers for school districts. Where teacher education is not part of the accountability or financial regime for schools, then partnering in teacher education may not be a priority for individual schools.

During the research visits, I noted several initiatives developed to build and sustain productive teacher education partnerships. In some cases, these were included in programme validation and accreditation requirements, in terms of requiring the development of authentic partnerships and through evidencing engagement with community groups. Moreover, considerable effort goes into working with school partners to consider the sorts of support that new teachers need as they enter the profession. However, within this work there are three main tensions:

–   Concerns around how schools are remunerated for the additional work that placements and mentoring new teachers can entail;

- Differences in perceptions between schools and universities as to what is required within teacher education, and what constitutes an acceptable teacher education candidate or graduate;

- Differences in perceptions as to who holds the power within teacher education particularly in relation to entry to the profession, and the distribution of (potential) new teachers in areas of need.

In New Zealand, Normal Schools are paid directly by central funding for the teacher education work they undertake. In Queensland, my site visit coincided with a renegotiation with teacher unions about the direct payment to teachers for student teacher supervision. The form of remuneration whether it comes out of programme fees or central funding, and whether it goes directly to the school, teacher or is overseen by the School Board or District has implications for the financial viability of teacher education as an activity within the university and also for the participation of schools.

Similarly, there can be a tension between universities and their partners as to what should be privileged in teacher education: whether the focus should be on what is learnt on practicum, the development of transferable skills, and the relevance of theoretical or academic knowledge. In several sites, teacher educators I spoke to emphasized how practice was central to learning to teach, and many of the schools I visited declared how important they felt the university's contribution and expertise was. However, there were also tensions expressed: teacher educators being out of touch with the rapid pace of change in schools, a disconnect between theory and practice, and a tension between what student teachers needed and what the course provided. A significant tension was also about the responsibility for the quality of teacher education, and whether this was held by the university or school partner. Whilst schools were partners, there was little long-term impact for them if their participation was weak (perhaps other than recruitment of future teachers). Schools wanted to be fully consulted and involved, and in some incidences were fully integrated into accreditation panels. However, in other cases, schools were distant from the challenges facing universities and unaware of why changes were being made. As an illustrative example, as partnerships reviewed arrangements around placements and practicums, school preferences for timing and duration might not fit in with university schedules, or the needs of a changing student population (including a shift to part-time students and career changers). Partnership maintenance was an extremely important but time-consuming aspect of teacher education, and one that rarely gets recognized or rewarded (Ellis & McNicholl, 2015). These tensions where often located within the different perceptions of what being a teacher meant, what was important, and what needed to be prioritized within a quality teacher education programme. Even in established partnerships maintaining a share vision was an ongoing process that required maintenance.

Teacher education is likely to continue to need to adapt as changes happen across the education space; particularly as school practices change, as our understanding of learning and teaching deepens, as student needs change, and as the organizations involved experience changes in both their working arrangements and legislative environment. These changes are inevitable, and some may be unpredictable. Whilst united action against policy shifts and accountability measures that divert attention are important, it is how teacher educators respond to these changes that will influence the quality of the teacher education experience.

Adaptivity in recent times

Never has this been truer than through the experience of teacher education programmes during the Covid-19 pandemic. The closure of some schools and universities and the pivot to online teaching for many presented very real challenges for teacher education programmes. There are many accounts of what changes were necessary and what adjustments were made during this period in order to support the ongoing development of new teachers (see the editorials of special issues on this topic in *Journal for the Education of Teachers*, Mutton, 2020, and the *European Journal of Teacher Education*, Flores and Swennen, 2020). Many of these adaptations include:

- Being taught online;
- Having to teach online (and having learnt to teach in this way, converting to teaching in face to face classrooms);
- Knowing when to use asynchronous and synchronous experiences;
- The use of digital fieldtrips and virtual excursions;
- Using mixed reality simulations and 360 degree media;
- Considering the impact of the digital divide and developing an understanding of digital citizenship;
- Working with parents, and handling criticism when teaching remotely;
- Establishing presence and ensuring engagement in online learning environments;
- Undertaking informal and formal assessments online;
- Observing teaching and being observed and assessed remotely.

In addition, teacher education had to consider new perspectives on the broader social and community function of schools, access and participation issues and dealing with public criticism and participating in debate.

As the world moves into a new stage of 'living with' the pandemic, issues of 'lost' learning, the legacy of poverty and differentiated access issues and the challenges of transitioning from online learning back to classroom and school spaces present a different set of challenges for teachers and for teacher educators. Necessity has required innovation and the rapid development of new skills, often within an unhelpful or absent policy environment. This has therefore been a period of profound adaptivity.

However, research (Brooks, McIntyre, & Mutton, 2021) suggests that pandemic-related shifts may not last, and there is a danger that as life returns to a sense of normality so teacher education, and the policies that drive it, may revert back to how it was before the pandemic. The lesson here, I would argue, is about leadership. In the examples given above on adaptive teacher education expertise, teacher educators have demonstrated leadership in managing the process of change and ensuring that decisions made are for the benefit of new teachers. This is the same process that drove many of the adaptations made during the pandemic. Leadership in this vein, is not just about taking control, but about making decisions based on what is important. The model of teacher education practice reflects that adaptivity can reflect a quality teacher education which does more than respond to a series of metrics or indicators derived from an accountability agenda or a governance regime. Adaptivity needs to be underpinned by a perspective on priorities about what would really make a difference. This is an understanding of education as transformation, built on a set of values and understandings about teaching, the societal needs that it serves and the role communities expect it to play, in other words, this understanding sees teacher education as being profoundly *educational*.

The model therefore, does not promote uniformity or indeed consistency, but recognizes that quality can be enacted in a variety of ways. As we have seen throughout this book, quality is a contested concept, conceptualized variously. One person's interpretation of what needs to be done and what is possible will depend on what they consider quality education to be, what a quality teacher or quality teaching looks like, what sort of teacher education they are referring to, and what they consider good practice in teacher education to be. The model reflects this nuanced approach to understanding quality: by recognizing that transformational pedagogy is possible even when some aspects of the teacher education infrastructure, or practice environments make transformation challenging. In other words, quality teacher education is possible in these different circumstances and contexts. Barriers to ideal practice will always be in place, but that need not prevent teacher education and teacher educators from striving for transformation. It also does not prevent teacher educators working collaboratively and strategically to counter narratives that will be threats to quality, or to speak out against policy agendas which are threats to quality. These actions are necessary too!

The model also recognizes that some aspects of what might be considered high-quality provision, such as the availability of 'ideal' candidates, or particular types of partnership, may be outside of the immediate remit of the teacher educator or programme. A high-quality programme will be one that addresses that problem specifically and in an informed way, such as through either considering how to support new teachers to be the best teachers they can be, or by seeking alternative ways to attract and accommodate different types of applicants. Teacher education provision will always need to adapt to reflect changing social and educational contexts.

Policy influences on teacher education will continue but will likely change (particularly as the world recovers from the Covid-19 pandemic); more quality conundrums will appear as others subside. Teacher education will need to adapt to these changing circumstances, and to do so will require detailed knowledge of the site and situation (situated knowledge), opportunities and developments in the field itself and how they might be gainfully deployed (adaptive teacher education expertise) and what possibilities there are for affective change (capacity to change). Moreover, high-quality teacher education will need to consider how these elements are inter-dependent and contingent upon each other.

Chapter 4 outlined how a research-orientated approach to teacher education has the capacity for high-quality outcomes and experiences. I would like to suggest that the same is true for a research orientation to understanding quality in teacher education itself. As the ways in which teacher education is conceptualized change, there is a need for professional teacher educators to draw upon research to lift it beyond the notion of technical training, and to place even greater emphasis on the educational dimension outlined here as transformation. Teacher 'training' or teacher 'preparation', as a form of professional training is distinctively different to teacher 'education'. The role of research is not just to inform about 'best practices' or 'what works' but to contribute to a body of knowledge that may inform decision-making and to support critical situational judgement. In the 'white heat' of action, teacher educators may not realize they are drawing on research-based knowledge but will be drawing on their understanding of a situation. To be prepared to make these situational judgements requires knowledge, and teacher educators need access to a variety of ideas and knowledges in order to develop that knowledge base. All educators need a variety of ideas and knowledges so they can develop their understanding of professional practice. It is this that underpins quality in teacher education when it is viewed through the lens of transformation.

REFERENCES

Adams, P., & McLennan, C. (2021). Towards initial teacher education quality: epistemological considerations. *Educational Philosophy and Theory*, 53(6), 644–54. doi:10.1080/00131857.2020.1807324

Adhikary, R. W., & Lingard, B. (2017). A critical policy analysis of 'Teach for Bangladesh': a travelling policy touches down. *Comparative Education*, 54(2), 181–202. doi:10.1080/03050068.2017.1360567

Alexander, R. J. (2015). Teaching and learning for all? The quality imperative revisited. *International Journal of Educational Development*, 40, 250–8. doi.org/10.1016/j.ijedudev.2014.11.012

Anderson, G. L., & Herr, K. (2011). Scaling up 'evidence-based' practices for teachers is a profitable but discredited paradigm. *Educational Researcher*, 40(6), 287–9. doi:10.3102/0013189X11417619

Ball, S. J. (1990). *Politics and policy making in education: explorations in policy sociology*. London: Routledge.

Ball, S. J. (2003). The teacher's soul and the terrors of performativity. *Journal of Education Policy*, 18(2), 215–28. doi:10.1080/0268093022000043065

Ball, S. J. (2008). Performativity, privatisation, professionals and the state. In B. Cunningham (Ed.), *Exploring Professionalism* (pp. 50–72). London: Bedford Way Papers.

Ball, S., Maguire, M., Braun, A., Perryman, J., & Hoskins, K. (2012). Assessment technologies in schools: 'deliverology' and the 'play of dominations'. *Research Papers in Education*, 27(5), 513–33. doi:10.1080/02671522.2010.550012

Barber, M. (2007). *Instruction to deliver: Tony Blair, public services and the challenge of achieving targets*. London: Politico's.

Barber, M., & Mourshed, M. (2007). *How the world's best-performing schools systems come out on top*. London: McKinsey & Company.

Barnes, M. (2021). Framing teacher quality in the Australian media: the circulation of key political messages? *Educational Review*, 1–17. doi:10.1080/00131911.2021.1907317

Barnes, M., Quiñones, G., & Berger, E. (2021). Constructions of quality: Australian Childhood Education and Care (ECEC) services during COVID-19. *Teachers and Teaching*, 1–18. doi:10.1080/13540602.2021.1979510

Bartell, T., Floden, R., & Richmond, G. (2018). What data and measures should inform teacher preparation? Reclaiming accountability. *Journal of Teacher Education*, *69*(5), 426–8. doi:10.1177/0022487118797326

Baxan, V., & Broad, K. (2017). *Graduate initial teacher education – a literature review*. Retrieved from Toronto: https://www.oise.utoronto.ca/mtvisioning/UserFiles/File/Literature_Review_Chapter_1_Final.pdf

Bennett, T., Grossberg, L., & Morris, M. (2005). *New keywords. A revised vocabulary of culture and society*. Oxford: Blackwell Publishing.

Biesta, G. (2007). Why 'what works' won't work: evidence-based practice and the democratic deficit in educational research. *Educational Theory*, *57*(1), 1–22. doi:doi.org/10.1111/j.1741-5446.2006.00241.x

Biesta, G. (2012). Receiving the gift of teaching: from 'learning from' to 'being taught by'. *Studies in Philosophy and Education*, *32*(5), 449–61. doi:10.1007/s11217-012-9312-9

Biesta, G. (2019). Reclaiming teaching for teacher education: towards a spiral curriculum. *Beijing International Review of Education*, *1*(2–3), 259–72. doi:10.1163/25902539-00102015

Biesta, G., Takayama, K., Kettle, M., & Heimans, S. (2021). Teacher education policy: part of the solution or part of the problem? *Asia-Pacific Journal of Teacher Education*, *49*(5), 467–70. doi:10.1080/1359866x.2021.1992926

Bourke, T., Ryan, M., & Lidstone, J. (2012). Reclaiming professionalism for geography education: defending our own territory. *Teaching and Teacher Education*, *28*(7), 990–8. doi:https://doi.org/10.1016/j.tate.2012.05.005

Brooks, C. (2021). *Initial teacher education at scale: quality conundrums*. London: Routledge.

Brooks, C., McIntyre, J., & Mutton, T. (2021). Teacher education policy making during the pandemic: shifting values underpinning change in England? *Teachers and Teaching*, 1–18. doi:https://doi. org/10.1080/13540602.2021.1997984

Brouwer, N., & Korthagen, F. (2005). Can teacher education make a difference? *American Educational Research Journal*, 42(1), 153–224. doi:https://doi.org/10.3102/00028312042001153

Brown, T. (2017). *Teacher education in England: a critical interrogation of school-led training.* London: Routledge.

Burn, K., & Mutton, T. (2013). *Review of research-informed clinical practice in teacher education, paper submitted to the BERA-RSA Inquiry.* London: BERA/RSA.

Caperton, G., & Whitmire, R. (2012). *The achievable dream: College Board lessons on creating great schools.* New York, NY: College Board.

Carter, A. (2015). *Carter Review of Initial Teacher Training (ITT).* Retrieved from London: https://assets.publishing.service.gov. uk/government/uploads/system/uploads/attachment_data/ file/399957/Carter_Review.pdf

Cochran-Smith, M. (2004). The problem of teacher education. *Journal of Teacher Education*, 55(4), 295–9. doi:10.1177/0022487104268057

Cochran-Smith, M. (2005). Studying teacher education: what we know and need to know. *Journal of Teacher Education*, 56(4), 301–6. doi:https://doi.org/10.1177/0022487105280116

Cochran-Smith, M. (2020). Relocating teacher preparation to new graduate schools of education. *The New Educator*, 17(1), 1–20. doi:10.1080/1547688x.2020.1814466

Cochran-Smith, M. (2021). Exploring teacher quality: international perspectives. *European Journal of Teacher Education*, 1–14. doi:10.1080/02619768.2021.1915276

Cochran-Smith, M., Carney, M. C., Keefe, E. S., Burton, S., Chang, W.-C., Fernández, M. B., … Baker, M. (2018). *Reclaiming accountability in teacher education.* New York: Teachers College Press.

Cochran-Smith, M., Keefe, E. S., Carney, M. C., Sanchez, J. G., Olivo, M., & Smith, R. J. (2020). Teacher preparation at New Graduate Schools of Education; studying a controversial innovation. *Teacher Education Quarterly*, 47(2), 8–37. https:// www.jstor.org/stable/26912665

Cochran-Smith, M., & Zeichner, K. M. (2005). *Studying teacher education: the report of the AERA Panel on Research and Teacher Education.* Mahwah, NJ: Lawrence Erlbaum Associates.

A Community of inquiry (2018). *Keywords; for further consideration and particularly relevant to academic life, especially as it concerns disciplines, inter-disciplinary endeavor and modes of resistance to the same*. Princeton, NJ: Princeton University Press.

Connell, R. (2009). Good teachers on dangerous ground: towards a new view of teacher quality and professionalism. *Critical Studies in Education, 50*(3), 213–29. doi:10.1080/17508480902998421

Crawford-Garrett, K., Rauschenberger, E., & Thomas, M. A. (2020). Examining teach for all: An introduction. In Matthew A.M. Thomas, Emilee Rauschenberger, Katherine Crawford-Garrett (Eds.), *Examining Teach for All* (pp. 3–12). London: Routledge.

Darling-Hammond, L. (2006). *Powerful teacher education: lessons from exemplary programs*. San Francisco: John Wiley & Sons.

Darling-Hammond, L. (2017). Teacher education around the world: what can we learn from international practice? *European Journal of Teacher Education, 40*(3), 291–309. doi:10.1080/02619768.2 017.1315399

Darling-Hammond, L. (2021). Defining teaching quality around the world. *European Journal of Teacher Education*, 1–14. doi:10.108 0/02619768.2021.1919080

Darling-Hammond, L., & Berry, B. (1999). Recruiting teachers for the 21st century: the foundation for educational equity. *The Journal of Negro Education, 68*(3), 254–79. doi:10.2307/2668100

Darling-Hammond, L., Macdonald, M. B., Snyder, J., Whitford, B. L., Ruscoe, G., & Fickel, L. (2000). *Studies of excellence in teacher education: preparation at the graduate level*. Washington DC: ATCEE.

Day, C. (2019). Policy, teacher education and the quality of teachers and teaching. *Teachers and Teaching, 25*(5), 501–6. doi:10.1080/ 13540602.2019.1651100

Department for Education (2010). *The importance of teaching* (9780101798020). Retrieved from London: https://assets. publishing.service.gov.uk/government/uploads/system/uploads/ attachment_data/file/175429/CM-7980.pdf

Department for Education (2019). *ITT core content framework*. Retrieved from London: https://assets.publishing.service.gov. uk/government/uploads/system/uploads/attachment_data/ file/919166/ITT_core_content_framework_.pdf.

Department for Education (2021). *Initial teacher training (ITT) market review report*. Retrieved from London: https://assets.

publishing.service.gov.uk/government/uploads/system/uploads/attachment_data/file/999621/ITT_market_review_report.pdf

Department for Education (2022). *Delivering worldclass teacher development: Policy paper*. Retrieved from London: https://assets.publishing.service.gov.uk/government/uploads/system/uploads/attachment_data/file/1059686/Delivering_world_class_teacher_development_policy_paper.pdf

Edwards-Groves, C., & Grootenboer, P. (2015). Praxis and the theory of practice architectures: resources for re-envisioning English education. *Australian Journal of Language and Literacy*, *38*(3), 150–61.

Ellis, V. (2019). Teacher education in England: a critical interrogation of school-led training. *Journal of Education for Teaching*, *45*(3), 365–7. doi:10.1080/02607476.2019.1607083

Ellis, V., Maguire, M., Trippestad, T. A., Liu, Y., Yang, X., & Zeichner, K. (2015). Teaching other people's children, elsewhere, for a while: the rhetoric of a travelling educational reform. *Journal of Education Policy*, *31*(1), 60–80. doi:10.1080/0268093 9.2015.1066871

Ellis, V., & McNicholl, J. (2015). *Transforming teacher education: reconfiguring the academic work*. London: Bloomsbury Publishing.

Ellis, V., Souto-Manning, M., & Turvey, K. (2018). Innovation in teacher education: towards a critical re-examination. *Journal of Education for Teaching*, *45*(1), 2–14. doi:10.1080/02607476.201 9.1550602

Ellis, V., & Spendlove, D. (2020). Mediating 'School Direct': the enactment of a reform policy by university-based teacher educators in England. *British Educational Research Journal*, *46*(5), 949–66. doi:10.1002/berj.3607

Ericsson, K.A., Krampe, R.T., & Tesch-Romer, C. (1993). The role of deliberate practice in the acquisition of expert performance. *Psychological Review 100*(3), 363–406. doi:10.1037//0033-295X.100.3.363

Evans, L. (2008). Professionalism, professionality and the development of education professionals. *British Journal of Educational Studies*, *56*(1), 20–38. doi:10.1111/j.1467-8527.2007.00392.x

Evans, L. (2011). The 'shape' of teacher professionalism in England: professional standards, performance management, professional development and the changes proposed in the 2010 White Paper. *British Educational Research Journal, 37*(5), 851–70. doi:10.108 0/01411926.2011.607231

Firestone, W. A., & Donaldson, M. L. (2019). Teacher evaluation as data use: what recent research suggests. *Educational Assessment, Evaluation and Accountability, 31*, 289–314. doi:10.1007/ s11092-019-09300-z

Flores, M. A., & Swennen, A. (2020). The COVID-19 pandemic and its effects on teacher education. *European Journal of Teacher Education, 43*(4), 453–6. doi:10.1080/02619768.2020.1824253

Francis, B., Hodgen, J., Craig, N., Taylor, B., Archer, L., Mazenod, A., … Connolly, P. (2019). Teacher 'quality' and attainment grouping: the role of within-school teacher deployment in social and educational inequality. *Teaching and Teacher Education, 77*, 183–92. doi:10.1016/j.tate.2018.10.001

Furlong, J. (2019). The universities and initial teacher education; challenging the discourse of derision. The case of Wales. *Teachers and Teaching, 25*(5), 574–88. doi:10.1080/13540602.2019.1652160

Gaertner, H., & Brunner, M. (2018). Once good teaching, always good teaching? The differential stability of student perceptions of teaching quality. *Educational Assessment, Evaluation and Accountability, 30*(2), 159–82. doi:10.1007/s11092-018-9277-5

Gallie, W. B. (1955). Essentially contested concepts. *Proceedings of the Aristotelian society 56*, 167–98.

Gewirtz, S., Maguire, M., Neumann, E., & Towers, E. (2019). What's wrong with 'deliverology'? Performance measurement, accountability and quality improvement in English secondary education. *Journal of Education Policy*, 1–26. doi:10.1080/02680 939.2019.1706103

Goldhaber, D. (2018). Evidence-based teacher preparation: policy context and what we know. *Journal of Teacher Education, 70*(2), 90–101. doi:10.1177/0022487118800712

Grossman, P. (2008). Responding to our critics: from crisis to opportunity in research on teacher education. *Journal of Teacher Education, 59*(1), 10–23. doi:10.1177/0022487107310748

Grossman, P. (2018). *Teaching core practices in teacher education.* Cambridge, MA: Harvard Education Publishing Group.

Grossman, P., Hammerness, K., & McDonald, M. (2009). Redefining teaching, re-imagining teacher education. *Teachers and Teaching, 15*(2), 273–89. doi:10.1080/13540600902875340

Grossman, P., Kavanagh, S., & Dean, C. (2018). The turn to practice in teacher education. In Grossman, Pam (Ed.), *Teaching core practices in teacher education* (pp. 1–13). Cambridge, MA: Harvard Education Press.

Grossman, P., Kazemi, E., Kavanagh, S. S., Franke, M., & Dutro, E. (2019). Learning to facilitate discussions: collaborations in practice-based teacher education. *Teaching and Teacher Education, 81*, 97–9. doi:10.1016/j.tate.2019.02.002

Grossman, P., & Pupik Dean, C. G. (2019). Negotiating a common language and shared understanding about core practices: the case of discussion. *Teaching and Teacher Education, 80*, 157–66. doi:10.1016/j.tate.2019.01.009

Halász, G., & Looney, J. (2019). Teacher professional competences and standards. Concepts and implementation. *European Journal of Education, 54*(3), 311–14. doi:10.1111/ejed.12351

Hammerness, K. (2013). Examining features of teacher education in Norway. *Scandinavian Journal of Educational Research, 57*(4), 400–19. doi:10.1080/00313831.2012.656285

Hammerness, K., & Klette, K. (2015). Indicators of quality in teacher education: looking at features of teacher education from an international perspective. In G. K. LeTendre & A. W. Wiseman (Eds.), *Promoting and Sustaining a Quality Teacher Workforce* (pp. 239–77). Bingley: Emerald Publishing.

Hanushek, E. (2002). Teacher quality. In L. Izumi & W. Evers (Eds.), *Teacher Quality* (pp. 1–12). Stanford, CA: Hoover Institute Press.

Harvey, L. (2007). The epistemology of quality. *Perspectives in Education, 25*(3), 1–13.

Harvey, L., & Knight, P. T. (1996). *Transforming higher education.* Bristol: Open University Press.

Henry, J. (2020). The cinematic pedagogies of underprepared teachers. *Teaching and Teacher Education, 89*, 102990. doi:10.1016/j.tate.2019.102990

Hiebert, J., Gallimore, R., & Stigler, J. W. (2002). A knowledge base for the teaching profession: what would it look like and how can we get one? *Educational Researcher, 31*(5), 3–15. doi:https://doi.org/10.3102/0013189X031005003

Hillage, J., Pearson, R., Anderson, A., & Tamkin, P. (1998). *Excellence in research on schools.* Sudbury: Department for Education and Employment.

Holmes Group (1986). *Tomorrow's teachers: a report of the Holmes Group.* East Lansing, MI: Holmes Group.

Hulme, M., Rauschenberger, E., & Meanwell, K. (2018). *Education symposium: creating a world class teaching system*. Manchester: Manchester Metropolitan University.

Ing, M., & Loeb, S. (2008). Assessing the effectiveness of teachers from different pathways: issues and results. In P. Grossman & S. Loeb (Eds.), *Alternative Routes to Teaching: Mapping the New Landscape of Teacher Education* (pp. 157–85). Cambridge, MA: Harvard Education Press.

Jerrim, J. (2011). *England's "plummeting" PISA test scores between 2000 and 2009: is the performance of our secondary school pupils really in relative decline*. Retrieved from: DoQSS Working Papers 11-09, Quantitative Social Science – UCL Social Research Institute, University College London.

Jones, J., & Ellis, V. (2019). Simple and complex views of teacher development. In *Oxford Education Research Encyclopedia*. Oxford: Oxford University Press.

Kennedy, A. (2018). Developing a new ITE programme: a story of compliant and disruptive narratives across different cultural spaces. *European Journal of Teacher Education, 41*(5), 638–53. doi:10.1080/02619768.2018.1529753

Kirby, S. N., McCombs, J. S., Barney, H., & Naftel, S. (2006). *Reforming teacher education; something old, something new*. Retrieved from Santa Monica: https://www.rand.org/content/dam/rand/pubs/monographs/2006/RAND_MG506.pdf

Kumashiro, K. K., Neal, L. V. I., & Sleeter, C. (2015). *Diversifying the teacher workforce: preparing and retaining highly effective teachers*. London: Routledge.

Labaree, D. F. (2006). *The trouble with ed schools*. New Haven: Yale University Press.

Lemov, D. (2010). *Teach like a champion: 49 techniques that put students on the path to college*. San Francisco: Jossey-Bass.

Ling, L. M. (2017). Australian teacher education: inside-out, outside-in, backwards and forwards? *European Journal of Teacher Education, 40*(5), 561–71. doi:10.1080/0261976 8.2017.1385599

Lortie, D. C. (1975). *Schoolteacher*. Chicago: University of Chicago Press.

Louden, W. (2008). 101 Damnations: the persistence of criticism and the absence of evidence about teacher education in Australia. *Teachers and Teaching: Theory and Practice, 14*(4), 357–68. doi:10.1080/13540600802037777

Mayer, D. (2017). Professionalizing teacher education. In *Oxford Research Encyclopedia of Education* (Vol. 1). doi:10.1093/acrefore/9780190264093.013.96

McCabe, C., Yanacek, H. & the Keywords project (2018). *Keywords for today. A 21st century vocabulary.* Oxford: Oxford University Press.

McNamara, O., Murray, J., & Phillips, R. (2017). *Policy and research evidence in the 'reform' of primary initial teacher education in England.* Cambridge Primary Review Trust Cambridge.

Menter, I. (2017). Teacher education research. In *Oxford Research Encyclopedia of Education.* Oxford: Oxford University Press.

Menter, I., Hulme, M., Elliot, D., Lewin, J., Baumfield, V., Britton, A., … McQueen, I. (2010). *Literature review on teacher education in the 21st century* (Scottish Government Social Research Ed.). University of Glasgow.

Mezirow, J. (2000). *Learning as Transformation: Critical Perspectives on a Theory in Progress.* The Jossey-Bass Higher and Adult Education Series. San Francisco, CA: Jossey-Bass Publishers.

Mockler, N. (2013). Teacher professional learning in a neoliberal age: audit, professionalism and identity. *Australian Journal of Teacher Education (Online)*, *38*(10), 35–47. doi:10.14221/ajte.2013v38n10.8

Moon, B. (2016). Building and agenda for reform of teacher education and training within the university. In B. Moon (Ed.), *Do Universities Have a Role in the Education and Training Teachers? An International Analysis of Policy and Practice* (pp. 251–62). Cambridge: Cambridge University Press.

Moore, A. (2004). *The good teacher: dominant discourses in teaching and teacher education.* London: RoutledgeFalmer.

Mutton, T. (2020). Teacher education and Covid-19: responses and opportunities for new pedagogical initiatives. *Journal of Education for Teaching*, 1–3. doi:10.1080/02607476.2020.1805189

Netolicky, D. M. (2019). *Transformational professional learning: making a difference in schools.* Abingdon: Routledge.

New Zealand Ministry of Education (2017). *Teacher registration and certification policy review.* Retrieved from https://teachingcouncil.nz/content/teacher-registration-and-certification-policy-review.

Noell, G. H., Burns, J. M., & Gansle, K. A. (2018). Linking student achievement to teacher preparation: emergent challenges in implementing value added assessment. *Journal of Teacher Education*, 70(2), 128–38. doi:10.1177/0022487118800708

O'Flaherty, J., & Beal, E. M. (2018). Core competencies and high leverage practices of the beginning teacher: a synthesis of the literature. *Journal of Education for Teaching*, 44(4), 461–78. doi:10.1080/02607476.2018.1450826

O'Neill, O. (2013). Intelligent accountability in education. *Oxford Review of Education*, 39(1), 4–16. doi:10.1080/03054985.2013.764761

OECD (2005). *Teachers matter: attracting, developing and retaining effective teachers*. Paris: Organisation for Economic Co-operation and Development (OECD) Publishing.

Orchard, J., & Winch, C. (2015). *What training do teachers need? Why theory is necessary to good teaching*. PESGB: Salisbury.

Pachler, N. (2013). Interesting times' or teacher education and professionalism in a 'brave new world. In M. Evans (Ed.), *Teacher Education and Pedagogy: Theory, Policy and Practice* (pp. 23–40). Cambridge: Cambridge University Press.

Paul, L., Louden, B., Elliott, M., & Scott, D. (2021). *Next steps: report of the quality initial teacher education review*. Retrieved from Canberra: https://apo.org.au/sites/default/files/resource-files/2021-06/apo-nid312866.pdf

Philip, T. M., Souto-Manning, M., Anderson, L., Horn, I., Carter Andrews, D. J., Stillman, J., & Varghese, M. (2018). Making justice peripheral by constructing practice as 'core': how the increasing prominence of core practices challenges teacher education. *Journal of Teacher Education*, 70(3), 251–64. doi:10.1177/0022487118798324

Pring, R. (2017). Research and the undermining of teacher education. In M. A. Peters (Ed.), *A Companion to Research in Teacher Education* (pp. 609–20). Dordrecht: Springer.

Rauschenberger, E., Adams, P., & Kennedy, A. (2017). *Measuring quality in initial teacher education: a literature review for Scotland's MQuITE Study* (S. C. o. D. o. E. (scde.ac.uk) Ed.). Edinburgh: Scottish Council of Deans of Education (scde.ac.uk).

Richert, A. E. (1997). Teaching teachers for the challenge of change. In J. Loughran & T. Russell (Eds.), *Teaching about Teaching* (pp. 73–94). London: The Falmer Press.

Sachs, J. (2003). *The activist teaching profession*. Maidenhead: Open University Press.

Sachs, J. (2015). Teacher professionalism: why are we still talking about it? *Teachers and Teaching, 22*(4), 413–25. doi:10.1080/135 40602.2015.1082732

Sahlberg, P. (2010). Educational change in Finland. In Hargreaves, A., Lieberman, A., Fullan, M., Hopkins, D. (Eds.), *Second international handbook of educational change* (pp. 323–48). Dordrecht: Springer.

Schorr, J. (2013). A revolution begins in teacher prep. *Stanford Social Innovation Review, 11*(1). Retrieved from https://ssir.org/pdf/Winter_2013_A_Revolution_Begins_in_Teacher_Prep.pdf

See, B. H., & Gorard, S. (2019). Why don't we have enough teachers?: A reconsideration of the available evidence. *Research Papers in Education*, 1–27. doi:10.1080/02671522.2019.1568535

Sims, S. (2021). *Making good on the ITT market review*. Retrieved from London: https://www.gatsby.org.uk/uploads/education/reports/pdf/itt-reform-expert-perspectives-2021.pdf

Skedsmo, G., & Huber, S. G. (2019). Measuring teaching quality: some key issues. *Educational Assessment, Evaluation and Accountability, 31*(2), 151–3. doi:10.1007/s11092-019-09299-3

Sleeter, C. (2019). Considering core assumptions about what it means to teach. *Teachers College Record, 121*, 1–4. doi:https://doi.org/10.1177/016146811912100609

Sloat, E., Amrein-Beardsley, A., & Holloway, J. (2018). Different teacher-level effectiveness estimates, different results: inter-model concordance across six generalized value-added models (VAMs). *Educational Assessment, Evaluation and Accountability, 30*(4), 367–97. doi:10.1007/s11092-018-9283-7

Smith, B. A. (2015). "If you cannot live by our rules, if you cannot adapt to this place, I can show you the back door." A Response to New forms of teacher education: connections to charter schools and their approaches. *Democracy and Education, 23*(1), 13. https://democracyeducationjournal.org/home/vol23/iss1/13

Smith, I., Brisard, E., & Menter, I. (2007). Models of partnership developments in initial teacher education in the four components of the United Kingdom: recent trends and current challenges. *Journal of Education for Teaching, 32*(2), 147–64. doi:10.1080/02607470600655136

Stitzlein, S. M., & West, C. K. (2014). New forms of teacher education: Connections to charter schools and their approaches. *Democracy and Education, 22*(2), 2. https://democracyeducationjournal.org/home/vol22/iss2/2

Stobart, G. (2008). *Testing times; the uses and abuses of assessment*. Abingdon: Routledge.

Tao, S. (2016). *Transforming teacher quality in the global south: using capabilities and causality to re-examine teacher performance*. Hampshire: Palgrave Macmillian.

Tatto, M. T. (2021). Developing teachers' research capacity: the essential role of teacher education. *Teaching Education*, *32*(1), 27–46. doi:10.1080/10476210.2020.1860000

Tatto, M. T., Burn, K., Menter, I., Mutton, T., & Thompson, I. (2017). *Learning to teach in England and the United States: the evolution of policy and practice*. Abingdon: Routledge.

Tatto, M. T., Richmond, G., & Carter Andrews, D. J. (2016). The research we need in teacher education. *Journal of Teacher Education*, *67*(4), 247–50. doi:10.1177/0022487116663694

Teacher Education Exchange (2017). *Teacher Development 3.0; How we can transform the professional education of teachers*. London: Teacher Education Exchange.

Thomas, M. A., Rauschenberger, E., & Crawford-Garrett, K. (2020). *Examining teach for all: international perspectives on a growing global network*. Abingdon: Routledge.

Vagi, R., Pivovarova, M., & Barnard, W. (2019). Dynamics of preservice teacher quality. *Teaching and Teacher Education*, *85*, 13–23. doi:10.1016/j.tate.2019.06.005

van der Lans, R. M. (2018). On the 'association between two things': the case of student surveys and classroom observations of teaching quality. *Educational Assessment, Evaluation and Accountability*, *30*(4), 347–66. doi:10.1007/s11092-018-9285-5

van der Schaaf, M., Slof, B., Boven, L., & De Jong, A. (2019). Evidence for measuring teachers' core practices. *European Journal of Teacher Education*, *42*(5), 675–94. doi:10.1080/02619 768.2019.1652903

Veltri, B. T. (2010). *Learning on other people's kids: becoming a teach for America teacher*. Charlotte: IAP.

Watson, C. (2018). From accountability to digital data: the rise and rise of educational governance. *Review of Education*, *7*(2), 390–427. doi:10.1002/rev3.3125

Whiting, C., Whitty, G., Menter, I., Black, P., Hordern, J., Parfitt, A., … Sorensen, N. (2018). Diversity and complexity: becoming a teacher in England in 2015–2016. *Review of Education*, *6*(1), 69–96. doi:10.1002/rev3.3108

Williams, R. (1976). *Keywords: a vocabulary of culture and society.* London, UK: Fontana.

Zeichner, K. (2016). *Independent teacher education programs: apocryphal claims, illusory evidence.* Boulder, CO: National Education Policy Center. Retrieved from http://nepc.colorado.edu/publication/teacher-education

Zeichner, K. (2017). *The struggle for the soul of teacher education.* Abingdon: Routledge.

Zhao, Y. (2018). The changing context of teaching and implications for teacher education. *Peabody Journal of Education, 93*(3), 295–308. doi:10.1080/0161956x.2018.1449896

Zumwalt, K., & Craig, E. (2005). Teachers' characteristics: research on the indicators of quality. In M. Cochran-Smith & K. Zeichner (Eds.), *Studying Teacher Education: The Report of the AERA Panel on Research and Teacher Education* (pp. 157–260). Washington, DC: American Educational Research Association.

INDEX